The Parish of Edenderry

ST. MARY'S
EDENDERRY, CO. OFFALY
PHONE (0405) 32352

THE FAITH OF ST. MARY'S PARISH has been celebrated through many centuries, with such notable milestones as the foundation of the Monastery of St. Colmcille at Ballinakill in the 6th/7th century, the Franciscan Monastery at Monasteroris in the 14th century, the Penal Day Chapel in Cokery Lane in the 17th/18th century, the Church in Killane in 1816, to the present, St. Mary's opened in 1919.

Here we continue the tradition of the celebration of the Liturgy, "the summit toward which the activity of the Church is directed; at the same time it is the foundation from which all her power flows. For the goal of apostolic works is that all who are made sons and daughters of God through faith and baptism should come together to praise God in the midst of his Church, to take part in the Sacrifice and to eat the Lord's supper. The Liturgy in its turn inspires the faithful to become of one heart in love… *it prays that they may grasp by deed what they hold by creed'.* " (Vatican 2)

So our mission is to bring all our people together as the people of God, sharing the Bread of Life and living the law of love through service to all our neighbours.

St. Mary's has a strong musical tradition and our Liturgies are enhanced by excellent choirs.

The future of our parish can be enriched by drawing example from and building on the strong faith and practice of past and present generations. Our parish population is set to grow rapidly over the next five years and one of the challenges facing us is to welcome and integrate new families into our community. Our welcome should be warm and inclusive, encouraging all to use their various gifts and talents to strengthen the faith of all as we gather as one around the table of the Eucharist.

Rt. Rev. Mgr. John McDonald

Rev. Laurence Malone

BACKGROUND:
Church at Killane, 1816

The Churches of Kildare and Leighlin

2000 A.D.

DRAWINGS AND RESEARCH BY

JOHN DUFFY

EDITED BY

JOHN MCEVOY

The Diocese of Kildare and Leighlin

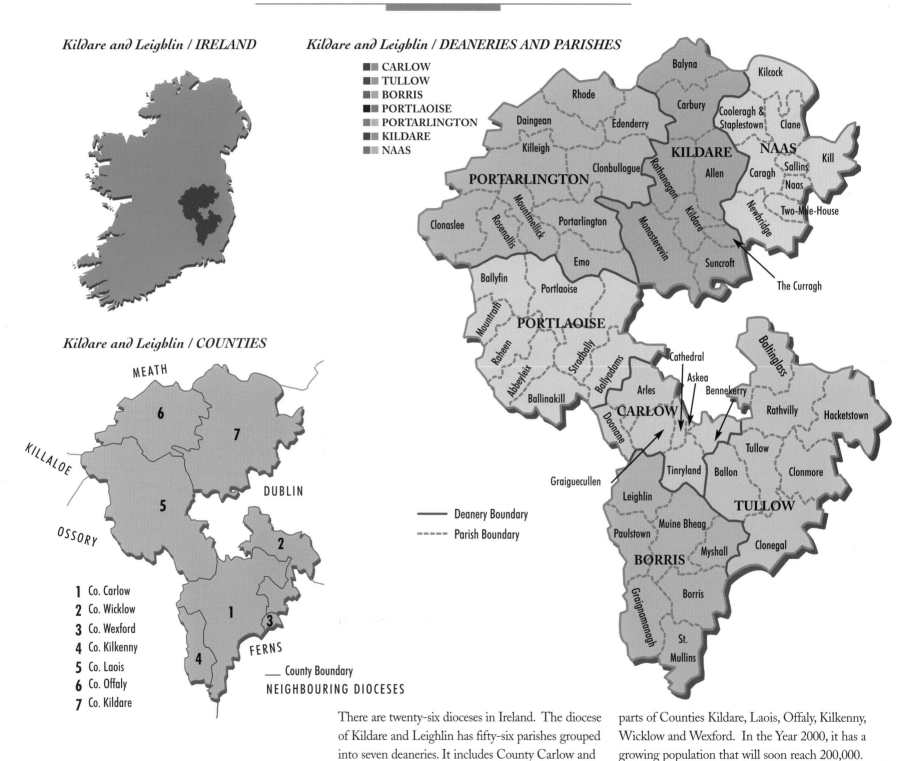

Kildare and Leighlin / IRELAND

Kildare and Leighlin / DEANERIES AND PARISHES

- CARLOW
- TULLOW
- BORRIS
- PORTLAOISE
- PORTARLINGTON
- KILDARE
- NAAS

Balyna · Kilcock · Rhode · Carbury · Cooleragh & Staplestown · Clane · Daingean · Edenderry · KILDARE · NAAS · Killeigh · Clonbullogue · Rathangan · Allen · Kill · PORTARLINGTON · Sallins · Caragh · Naas · Clonaslee · Rosenallis · Mountmellick · Portarlington · Monsterevin · Kildare · Newbridge · Two-Mile-House · Emo · Suncroft · Ballyfin · Portlaoise · The Curragh · Mountrath · PORTLAOISE · Raheen · Stradbally · Cathedral · Baltinglass · Abbeyleix · Ballyadams · Askea · Ballinakill · Arles · Bennekerry · Rathvilly · Hacketstown · CARLOW · Tullow · Doonane · Clonmore · Graiguecullen · Tinryland · Ballon · Leighlin · TULLOW · Muine Bheag · Clonegal · Paulstown · Myshall · BORRIS · Borris · Graignamanagh · St. Mullins

—— Deanery Boundary

---- Parish Boundary

Kildare and Leighlin / COUNTIES

MEATH · KILLALOE · OSSORY · DUBLIN · FERNS

1 Co. Carlow
2 Co. Wicklow
3 Co. Wexford
4 Co. Kilkenny
5 Co. Laois
6 Co. Offaly
7 Co. Kildare

— County Boundary

NEIGHBOURING DIOCESES

There are twenty-six dioceses in Ireland. The diocese of Kildare and Leighlin has fifty-six parishes grouped into seven deaneries. It includes County Carlow and parts of Counties Kildare, Laois, Offaly, Kilkenny, Wicklow and Wexford. In the Year 2000, it has a growing population that will soon reach 200,000.

Table of Contents

Credits 4

Foreword and Editor's Introduction 5

The History of Church Buildings in Kildare & Leighlin 6

John Duffy Biography 7

The History of the Diocese of Kildare & Leighlin 8

Carlow Deanery 9-22

CATHEDRAL, ASKEA, BENNEKERRY, ARLES, DOONANE, GRAIGUECULLEN, TINRYLAND

Tullow Deanery 23-40

TULLOW, BALLON, CLONEGAL, CLONMORE, RATHVILLY, BALTINGLASS, HACKETSTOWN

Borris Deanery 41-57

BORRIS, ST. MULLINS, GRAIGNAMANAGH, MYSHALL, MUINE BHEAG, PAULSTOWN, LEIGHLIN

Portlaoise Deanery 59-74

PORTLAOISE, STRADBALLY, BALLYADAMS, BALLINAKILL, ABBEYLEIX, RAHEEN, MOUNTRATH, BALLYFIN

Portarlington Deanery 75-94

PORTARLINGTON, EMO, MOUNTMELLICK, ROSENALLIS, CLONASLEE, KILLEIGH, CLONBULLOGUE, EDENDERRY, RHODE, DAINGEAN

Kildare Deanery 95-110

KILDARE, CURRAGH CAMP, SUNCROFT, MONASTEREVIN, ALLEN, CARBURY, BALYNA, RATHANGAN

Naas Deanery 111-127

NAAS, SALLINS, TWO-MILE-HOUSE, NEWBRIDGE, CARAGH, COOLERAGH, KILCOCK, CLANE, KILL

Specially Featured:

Carlow College and St. Mary's, Knockbeg 12

Early History of the Diocese of Leighlin 13

St. Patrick's Missionary Society, Kiltegan 35

Religious Orders and Congregations 45

Leighlin Cathedral (Church of Ireland) 58

Early History of the Diocese of Kildare 98

Kildare Cathedral (Church of Ireland) 99

Bibliography and Index 128

Special Thanks

TO THE FOLLOWING FOR ASSISTANCE IN THIS PUBLICATION:

Bishop Laurence Ryan and the clergy of the diocese, local historians,
and those who supplied old photographs and parish information,
and in particular the following: Jimmy O'Toole, Msgr. Brendan Byrne V.G.,
Robert Duffy, Thomas Sunderland (Photography), Brian Kelly, Mrs. Agnes Phelan,
Rev. Dean Robert Townley (Kildare), Rev. Ken Sherwood (Old Leighlin),
Fr. Andrew Keating (Kiltegan), Fr. Conn Ó Maoldhomhnaigh and Fr. Caoimhín Ó Néill.

Cover Picture: Cathedral of the Assumption, Carlow (1833).

DRAWINGS AND RESEARCH BY:
John DUFFY

EDITED BY:
John McEVOY

PROJECT MANAGER:
Bill KEMMY

COVER DESIGN:
Maria WALSHE

LAYOUT:
Juliette ROUSSEL

PUBLISHING DIRECTOR:
Christian RIEHL

DIRECTOR OF PUBLICATIONS:
Dr. Claude-Bernard COSTECALDE

PUBLISHING ASSISTANT:
Joëlle BERNHARD

PUBLISHED BY:
Éditions du Signe
1, rue Alfred Kastler
67038 Strasbourg, Cedex 2 – France
Tel: (33) 3 88 78 91 91
Fax (33) 3 88 78 91 99

©2001 Éditions du Signe
ISBN: 2-7468-0293.7
Printed in Italy by AGES Arti Grafiche

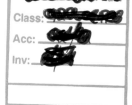

Foreword

CHURCH BUILDINGS are much more than mere physical structures. Each one is a public permanent statement of the faith of a community. They invite people to prayer and direct their minds and hearts from earth to heaven.

This book brings together for us the churches in every parish in Kildare and Leighlin in the year 2000. Each church is the place of celebration of significant events in the Christian journey of generations of local people from baptism to burial. All these generations speak through them to the people of the present day. The basic information given to us here about each church is limited but is very instructive – the date of origin and an outline of the history of the church. These apparently bare facts frame the life story of a faith community.

The timing of this production has a special significance. It is produced as one of our diocesan projects to mark the Great Jubilee Year of 2000. That year was a joyful celebration of the

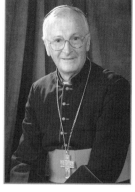

heritage of faith, which has been passed on to us of this generation. The book is a worthy memorial to the generations to whom we owe our faith and to whose sacrifices and strong faith we owe the churches throughout our diocese. As we enter on a new millennium they signal the way ahead for us. In order to keep alive the faith, which has flourished in the past, they call upon us to embark on the *new evangelisation* which Pope John Paul II has been calling for in recent years.

I congratulate John Duffy, Father John McEvoy and all whose combined efforts have resulted in this production. Its value will extend far beyond its contemporary interest. For many years to come it will be a rich source of information about the diocese of Kildare and Leighlin and every parish in it as we begin the third millennium of the Christian era.

Bishop Laurence Ryan

Editor's Introduction

THIS VOLUME attempts to capture in drawings and text something of the texture of life in the parishes of Kildare and Leighlin diocese. The drawings are all by John Duffy, who also researched the history of the churches and parishes of the Diocese. The present church buildings are the successors of innumerable structures, which have previously served for the gathering of people in worship. In some cases there has been continuity of worship on precisely the same site for a very long time. In most districts several different sites have served the worship needs of local communities.

Countless thousands of our ancestors have put energy and resources into providing for us beautiful and worthy places of worship. We wish to honour their memory through this compilation.

I wish to thank John Duffy and his wife Ann for their tireless work on the project. Sincere thanks to Dr. Claude Costecalde and his staff, particularly Sylvie and Joëlle, at Editions du Signe. It was a great pleasure to work with them.

Fr. John McEvoy

The History of Church Buildings in Kildare and Leighlin

THIS VOLUME details the 117 churches presently in use in the Diocese of Kildare & Leighlin, as well as a number of prominent religious establishments. Virtually all these buildings were constructed in the last three hundred years. Only the splendid 12th Century Duiske Abbey, now the Parish Church of Graignamanagh, remains from earlier times.

The rise and fall of church buildings were often dictated by political and religious upheavals - the Reformation, the later Penal Laws and subsequent Catholic Emancipation. Likewise, social realities, such as the huge population increase in the first half of the 19th Century, have greatly influenced the construction and location of churches. The most modern church in the diocese - Ballycane (1997) in Naas Parish - is a contemporary example of this process as it was provided to serve a fast-growing urban centre.

Church building in our diocese began with the ancient monasteries and their founders, two obvious examples being Brigid of Kildare and Laserian of Leighlin. Cogitosus, the 7th century biographer of St. Brigid, describes her double monastery in Kildare as a large and lofty structure with many windows and decorated with frescoes. Since that time numerous church buildings have come and gone, often to be replaced by finer and sturdier constructions.

The first churches were mostly humble structures of wood or wattle and daub. The stone structures that survive at ancient monastic sites belong to a later age. The earliest reliable reference to a stone church in Ireland is the year 788. The ancient Round towers, often over 100ft. tall, show the capabilities of our ancient builders. In the following centuries, building style held to the monastic tradition although some elaborate building did take place, chiefly in the Romanesque style. The surviving doorway at Killeshin (Co. Laois) reveals the accomplished craftsmanship of that period.

The arrival of the Continental monastic orders, particularly the Cistercians, was to greatly influence church architecture.

The Diocese of Leighlin has two outstanding examples of Cistercian architecture - Duiske Abbey (1204) on the banks of the River Barrow, and (the now ruined) Baltinglass Abbey (1148) beside the River Slaney. Their architectural style was late Romanesque, with the use of pointed arches, which later characterised the Gothic style.

The Reformation in the early 16th century profoundly changed religious life and the social order. Henry VIII's Act of Suppression, passed in 1536, heralded the dissolution of the monasteries and widespread confiscation of land. Catholic church building came to an abrupt halt, and existing establishments fell into decay.

The Penal Laws, which greatly curtailed the activity of the Catholic Church and particularly its clergy, continued until the late 1700's, when some concessions were granted. It is no surprise that church architecture from the time of Henry VIII to the 1800's is confined to rather modest buildings. During this period, Catholics attended Mass celebrated by fugitive priests, usually in remote places. Many parishes retain a tradition or knowledge of the Mass Rocks in their area.

A great symbol of the changing circumstances for the Catholic Church in Ireland was the foundation of Carlow College in 1782. Opened in 1793, it provided for the training of young men for the Professions and for the Priesthood. In 1892, the Lay College moved to St. Mary's, Knockbeg.

After Duiske Abbey, the oldest church still in use in this diocese is the Sacred Heart Church in Rathcoffey (Clane Parish, Co. Kildare), which dates from 1710. The building date for churches was often recorded on foundation stones. For the few where the precise date is not known an approximate date can be given.

The 116 churches still providing a place of worship from the last three hundred years can be divided into the following categories: - Ten are pre-1800; thirty-one are of the period 1800-1830; twenty-five were built 1831-1860; twenty date from 1861-1900; only five

*Duiske Abbey, Graignamanagh
and Irish Martyrs, Naas*

were erected between 1901-1950, while twenty-three were constructed after 1950.

The churches built after 1950 generally replaced old ones. Observing the construction dates of the old churches that were replaced, one notes that at least fourteen were built prior to 1830. If these had been maintained, the period 1800-1830 would account for almost 40% of the present number of churches in the diocese.

While Catholic Emancipation was not achieved until 1829, the number of churches built in the period 1800-1830 appears strangely high. It may be partly explained by population figures, which grew from about 5 million to over 8 million in the forty-seven years following the Act of Union (1800).

The architecture of that time was very basic, consisting of small rectangular-shaped stone buildings or the same barn-style with transepts (often added later) giving a cruciform appearance. A small number of larger barn-style churches were also built, such as Hacketstown (1803) and Kill (1821).

After Catholic Emancipation in 1829, more substantial churches began to appear, often in the revived Gothic style. The main period of magnificent churches in the diocese was 1860-1900. Although, some fine examples were built prior to this date, such as Naas (1827-1858), Carlow Cathedral (1828-1833) and Monasterevin (1847), the latter by architect William Deane Butler.

The characteristics of the Gothic Style are towers with tall thin spires, often flanked by four pointed pinnacles, and walls with battlement features. Rectangular in shape, the buildings have windows with pointed arches and simple tracery, usually an intersecting pattern. Unlike earlier churches of rubble stone, these buildings are of fine cut stone, often exquisitely carved.

The Gothic style was first employed by the Church of Ireland from the late 1700's and subsequently adopted by the Catholic Church. Augustus Welby Pugin (1812-1852), a self-taught English architect, was chiefly responsible for the Gothic revival in church building. In his short life he designed over 100 buildings, and was skilled in furnishings, stained glass, ceramics, wrought iron, wallpaper, and book illustration. He encouraged many architects such as J.J. McCarthy (Kilcock, Mountmellick).

Pugin's son, who went into partnership with Irish architect George Ashlin, was responsible for many of the late nineteenth century Gothic churches in Ireland, such as Arles (1868). Another notable architect of this period was William Hague (Abbeyleix, Clane, Rathvilly and others).

The period 1900-1950 witnessed the building of very few churches in the Diocese. The outstanding example of this period is St. Mary's in Edenderry (1919).

The modern era (after 1950) has seen the building of twenty-three churches. Some, such as Ballymany in Newbridge (1982) and Ballycane – already mentioned - were built to cater for fast growing towns, but in general, modern churches were erected to replace older buildings, such as those at Caragh (1960/1790), Killeigh (1971/1808), and Shanahoe (1966/1816).

In recalling the history of Church Buildings in this diocese, it is clear that our present places of worship belong to a great tradition and connect us with the earliest gatherings of Christian people in this land. We have inherited a tremendous legacy from those past generations. The beginning of the new millennium is a very opportune time to remember and to give thanks.

John Duffy

John Duffy is a native of Hacketstown, Co. Carlow. Educated at Hacketstown National School, Ring College, Co. Waterford, Dominican College, Newbridge, and Warrenstown Agricultural College, he spent some years farming and in the timber industry until he became a full-time artist in 1992. Self-taught, John specialises in pencil and pen and ink drawings. He lives in Tullow with his wife Ann and their four sons.

A BRIEF HISTORY OF THE DIOCESE OF KILDARE AND LEIGHLIN

THE FIRST BISHOP to govern Kildare and Leighlin, Mark Forstal, died in exile in Cashel in 1681. After just three years of the new arrangement, the clergy of Leighlin petitioned to have Leighlin annexed to Ossory. The petition was unsuccessful.

Edward Murphy who served as bishop (1715-1724) became Archbishop of Dublin (1724-1729). James Gallagher, bishop of Raphoe (1725-1737) was transferred to Kildare and Leighlin (1737-1751). His publication of *Sermons* went through several editions in Irish and English. He had composed them while, after an attempt on his life, he spent a year in a safe retreat on one of the islands on Lough Erne, Co. Fermanagh. In Kildare he resided in a cabin in the Kilmeague area of the present parish of Allen. Tradition holds that Dr Gallagher conducted a small seminary in the Bog of Allen. Rudimentary education was imparted to young men, they were ordained and then sent to the continent for their theological education.

James Keefe was bishop for 35 years (1752-1787). Initially he resided in Kilmeague area (Parish of Allen). The Green Lane in Robertstown West was referred to by old residents as 'Boreen Keefe' until recent times. He resided mainly at Tullow, Co. Carlow. When he was already eighty years old, after the passing of Luke Gardiner's Act of Relief of some penal laws regarding catholic schools in 1782, Bishop Keefe transferred to Carlow town to oversee the building of Carlow College for the education of both lay and ecclesiastical students. When he died the building was almost ready for occupation.

Richard O'Reilly, P.P. Kilcock and Co-adjutor to Dr. Keefe (1781-1783), became Co-adjutor and subsequently Archbishop of Armagh (1783-1818). The next bishop, Daniel Delany, had been Keefe's Co-adjutor since 1783. He oversaw Carlow College from its opening in 1793, appointing Dean Henry Staunton, P.P. of Carlow, to be the first President. Carlow College has had an illustrious history, preparing men for the professions in the Lay College up to 1892 and educating over 3,600 to serve in the priesthood both in Irish dioceses and abroad, particularly in the United States, Britain and Australia.

During his episcopacy, Daniel Delany founded two teaching orders, Brigidine Sisters (1807) and Patrician Brothers (1808). Their mother houses are in Tullow. Subsequently these congregations made foundations in several parishes of the diocese and in other English-speaking countries, notably in Australia. The Presentation Sisters came to Carlow town in 1811, leading to the founding of many convents in the whole diocese.

Peter Kenney S.J., who had studied in Carlow in 1801-1804, became in 1814 the founder and first Rector of Clongowes Wood College near Clane, Co. Kildare. This Jesuit College has ever since made an immense contribution to Irish secondary education.

After the short episcopacy of Michael Corcoran, who lived at Tullow, came the most famous bishop of the united diocese of Kildare and Leighlin. In 1819 at the age of 33, James Doyle, O.S.A., a professor at Carlow College since 1813, was consecrated bishop. His fifteen years were remarkable for the impact made at local and national level. He became well known for his writings under the initials, J.K.L. (James Kildare & Leighlin). He took on the political powers of his day and was in close contact with Daniel O'Connell in the fight for Catholic Emancipation. He completed the building of Carlow Cathedral in the years 1828-1833. Unfortunately his health deteriorated and he died in 1834, only months after the opening of his Cathedral. In 1825 Dr. Doyle moved to Braganza House (Carlow), which continued to be the episcopal residence until 1969.

Venerable Catherine McAuley, foundress of the Sisters of Mercy, opened St. Leo's Convent in Carlow in 1837. From there the first Mercy Sisters went to work in the United States in 1843 (initially in Pittsburgh) and in New Zealand in 1849 (at first in Auckland). Schools were opened in several parishes by teaching sisters and brothers throughout the nineteenth century. St. Mary's College, Knockbeg absorbed the Carlow Lay College in 1892 and is now a boarding and day school for boys.

Three long episcopates dominate the period 1856-1967: James Walshe (1856-1888), Patrick Foley (1896-1926) and Thomas Keogh (1936-1967). A Vincentian priest, James Lynch, was bishop in succession to Walshe (1888-1896). His main contribution related to the religious congregations of the diocese. During the episcopate of Matthew Cullen (1927-1936), the new Missionary Society of St. Patrick was established in the diocese at Kiltegan, Co. Wicklow. The contribution of the Kiltegan Fathers in many African countries as well as in other continents has been immense. The diocese has also had a missionary outreach over two centuries through the work of Carlow College and of the many religious congregations.

To Bishop Patrick Lennon (1968-1987) fell the lot of implementing the changes, resulting from the Second Vatican Council. He created several new parishes and blessed many new and renovated churches. A man of great prudence, he wisely guided the diocese through a period of great transformation.

The present bishop is a native of the most southerly parish, St Mullins, Co. Carlow: Laurence Ryan, whose episcopate began in December 1987. During the late twentieth century, proximity to Dublin has caused rapid growth in the diocesan population. In the same period the supply of diocesan priests has decreased considerably. The diocese expects the early years of the new millennium to be marked by the involvement of more lay people in the administrative work of its parishes.

CARLOW DEANERY

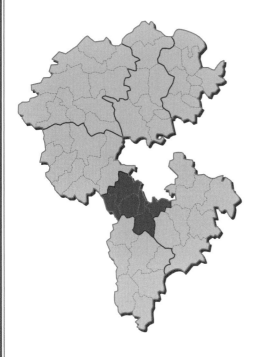

PARISHES

CATHEDRAL	10,11
ASKEA	14
BENNEKERRY	15
ARLES	16, 17
DOONANE	18, 19
GRAIGUECULLEN	20, 21
TINRYLAND	22

SPECIALLY FEATURED

Carlow College and St. Mary's, Knockbeg	12
Early History of the Diocese of Leighlin	13

Cathedral Parish, Carlow

PARISH PERSONNEL IN THE YEAR 2000

MOST REV. LAURENCE RYAN,
V. REV. GERARD AHERN, ADM.
REV. ANDREW LEAHY, C.C.
REV. GERRY CUSHEN, C.C.
REV. JOHN CUMMINS (IT CHAPLAIN)

V. REV. LAURENCE FLEMING P.E.
REV. CONOR O'REILLY, DEACON
REV. PATRICK BYRNE, DEACON
SR. DOLORES FITZGERALD, R.S.M.

CATHOLIC POPULATION: 8,000

Carlow Cathedral

CARLOW (CEATHARLACH, FOUR LAKES)

THE TRADITION OF THE LAKES, and perhaps the lakes themselves, existed in the late eighteenth century.

King Cormac, who died in 567, made a grant to St. Comgall of three towns in his territory, one of which was present-day Carlow, where the Saint established a monastic church. Brewer, in his "Beauties of Ireland," refers to an Abbey built by St. Kieran near Carlow c. 634. An old ecclesiastical building and burial ground survives at Castle Hill, Carlow, traditionally known as St. Mary's Abbey. St. Mary's Church of Ireland marks the site.

A chapel from the penal period existed between Carlow College and the Dublin Road. In 1787 Dr. Henry Staunton, Parish Priest of Carlow, built a sizeable Church on the later Cathedral site.

Bishop James Doyle ('J.K.L.') laid the foundation stone of the Cathedral on March 18th, 1828. Dr. Doyle is regarded by most historians as the outstanding Bishop of the 19th Century. Mr. Thomas Cobden, a noted 19th century architect, designed the Cathedral, which became the first to be built after Catholic Emancipation. He pioneered the Gothic revival in Ireland and designed many churches in the midlands. For the Cathedral he drew his inspiration from European examples, most notably the Beffroi Tower in Bruges.

Bishop James Warren Doyle (J. K. L.) (1819 - 1834)

The Cathedral was completed in 1833 at a cost of £9,000 and the old church was demolished. Part of its transept walls was retained and incorporated into the new structure. The greyish–blue stone used came from a quarry on the Carlow-Tullow Road. The white granite used came from Col. Bruen's quarry at Graiguenaspidogue. The oak for the great-framed roof came from nearby Oak Park. The Cathedral is a handsome mixture of gothic revival styles and was a tower of 151 ft. The windows are early medieval in style while the low pitched roof has a late medieval appearance.

The Cathedral was dedicated by Dr. Doyle on 1st Dec. 1833, and was initially sparsely furnished. In 1834, Dr. Doyle succumbed to a fatal disease, at the age of 48. His remains are buried in the Cathedral. In 1837, John Hogan of Tallow, Co. Waterford, won the commission for the memorial statue to Dr. James Doyle. It was finished in Rome in 1839 and placed in the Cathedral. Later a Holy Family Group, attributed to the same John Hogan, was added and may be seen beside the Marian altar.

Many refurbishments and improvements took place over the years. Dr. Michael Comerford, co-adjutor bishop and the noted diocesan historian, presented the great bell in 1889.

The Cathedral was consecrated on Nov. 30th 1933 by Bishop Matthew Cullen. Between 1949 and 1965 interior and exterior renovations were carried out.

Following a programme of refurbishment and renewal conducted under architect Richard Pierce and main contractor James Farrell (Construction Ltd.) the Cathedral was rededicated on Sunday 22nd June, 1997 in a ceremony performed by Bishop Laurence Ryan.

This most recent refurbishment cost £1,453,616. Several works of art were installed – the Ambo by Michael Burke; the altar and baptismal font by Michael Hoy; reliefs on confessionals by Philip Flanagan; work by Hughes sculptors; joinery work by Breffni Ireland and gilding by Susan Mulhall. The organ, one of the finest in the country, was completely overhauled at a cost of £38,894. This work was carried out by the Irish Organ Co., and the 2,000 pipes were cleaned and tuned by ear.

It is fitting that much of the stone for the refurbishment of the Cathedral came from quarries in Old Leighlin, where St. Laserian led the ancient diocese of Leighlin.

Carlow Cathedral

St. Patrick's College, Carlow & St. Mary's College, Knockbeg

CLERGY IN THE COLLEGES IN THE YEAR 2000

CARLOW COLLEGE

V. REV. CAOIMHÍN Ó NÉILL (PRESIDENT)
REV. JOHN MCEVOY (BURSAR/ REGISTRAR)
REV. CONN Ó MAOLDHOMHNAIGH
(DIRECTOR OF FORMATION)

KNOCKBEG COLLEGE

V. REV. DANIEL DUNNE (RECTOR)
REV. MÍCHEÁL MURPHY
REV. JOSEPH O'NEILL
(CHAPLAIN)

ST. PATRICK'S (CARLOW COLLEGE) IS SITUATED ON COLLEGE STREET. ITS ENTRANCE IS BESIDE CARLOW CATHEDRAL. ST. MARY'S (KNOCKBEG COLLEGE) HAS A RURAL SETTING ON THE CO. LAOIS SIDE OF THE RIVER BARROW, ABOUT TWO MILES FROM CARLOW TOWN AND CLOSE TO THE RUINS OF ST. FIACC'S MONASTERY AT SLEATY

The Façade of Knockbeg College (1908-1909)

THE HISTORY of the two Colleges is intertwined. Carlow College was founded by Bishop James Keefe in 1782, following the relaxation of Penal Laws restricting Catholic education. The first building of the College (costing £6,000) was built during the 1780's. Education commenced there on 1 October 1793, six years after the death of Bishop Keefe. From the start the College educated young men for the Professions (the Lay College) and for the Priesthood (the Seminary). In 1847 Knockbeg House was acquired by Bishop Francis Haly for Carlow College and it served until 1892 as a Preparatory School for boys (aged 8-12 years) wishing to enter Carlow College. In 1892, Knockbeg was enlarged and the Lay College transferred from St. Patrick's to St. Mary's. The front building in Knockbeg (illustrated) was provided in 1908-1909.

Between 1892 and 1978, St. Patrick's served exclusively as a Seminary for both home and foreign missions. From 1978 to 1996, The Irish Institute of Pastoral Liturgy (founded by Msgr. Seán Swayne) had its home in the South Wing of St. Patrick's.

Carlow College is now a private third-level Catholic College providing courses in Theology, Humanities and Social Studies to about 350 students, while Knockbeg College is a boarding and day Secondary School for about 250 boys.

Middle House in Carlow College has existed from opening day. In 1819, South Wing was opened to provide facilities for the Lay College. In the mid-1830's North Wing (New House) was added, improving facilities for worship, cooking, staff and student residences. The College Chapel of the Sacred Heart was added during the years 1885-1888. It was designed by the architect William Hague in the Hiberno-Romanesque style. The then President made a fund-raising trip to America to visit College alumni serving in Missions there. The cost of the new Chapel was £3,000.

Carlow College, founded by Bishop James Keefe in 1782

About 3,500 priests have been ordained from Carlow College. 1,150 of these have served in Irish Dioceses, while two-thirds of the total served in Dioceses all over the English-speaking world and other missions. Many thousands of others were educated there. St. Mary's, Knockbeg, has an intake of about sixty students per annum.

Architect Richard Hurley designed the re-ordering of Sacred Heart Chapel, Carlow College in 1969-1970. Again in 1977-1978 he was the architect for South Wing (including its Chapel), when it was prepared to house the Liturgy Institute.

Sacred Heart Chapel, Carlow College.

EARLY HISTORY OF THE DIOCESE OF LEIGHLIN

ST. LASERIAN (Molaise) was a grandson of Aidan, king of the Scots. He resisted being made chief of his clan and retired to Holy Island in the Firth of Clyde, Scotland. He then spent 14 years in Rome and studied under St Gregory the Great, who ordained him a priest and sent him back to Ireland. He settled in the monastery at Leighlin (Co. Carlow) founded by St Gobban. The controversy about the date of Easter raged at the time in Ireland. A synod on the subject was held at Leighlin in 630. Laserian succeeded Gobban as Abbot at about this time. He undertook a trip to Rome in 633 to get a resolution of the Easter controversy. Pope Honorius I consecrated Laserian bishop and appointed him legate to Ireland. He is credited with resolving the controversy for the southern half of Ireland. Leighlin may have had as many as 1500 monks at one stage. Laserian died in 639 and his feast as patron of the diocese is on 18th April. The church of Laserian was destroyed by fire in 1060. The present stone Cathedral (C. of I.) in Old Leighlin was commenced by Bishop Donatus in the years 1152-1181.

St. Fintan founded the famous monastery of Clonenagh (Co. Laois) in 548. It continued as a place of learning until the eleventh century. St. Mullins was the location of a significant monastic development and is named after its founder, Naomh Moling. Killeshin, Co. Laois has a beautifully preserved Romanesque doorway in the remains of its monastic church. Timahoe (Co. Laois) has a completely preserved Round Tower.

From the twelfth century new religious orders were established under the influence of the Normans. Leighlin diocese had three Cistercian foundations: Abbeyleix (1183), Baltinglass (1148) and Duiske Abbey (Graignamanagh, 1204). There were Carmelites in Leighlinbridge and Franciscans in Carlow town for several centuries.

In the Reformation period the succession of bishops was interrupted and Leighlin was governed by vicars general. A Spanish Franciscan, Francis de Ribera, would seem never to have set foot in Leighlin after his appointment in 1587. He died at Antwerp in 1604.

The last bishop of Leighlin was Edmund Dempsey O.P. (1642-1661). His episcopate coincided with the Confederacy of Kilkenny and the Cromwellian campaign in Ireland. He died in exile in Gallicia.

Medieval seal of St. Laserian's Cathedral -found in a bog near Clara, Co. Kilkenny.

Parish of Askea

PARISH TEAM IN THE YEAR 2000
V. REV. JOHN FITZPATRICK, ADM., V. F.
REV. GERARD BREEN, C.C.
REV. JOSEPH O'NEILL, C.C.
SR. JOAN PIERSE, I.B.V.M.

CATHOLIC POPULATION: 9,500

Holy Family Church, Askea.

DATE OF CHURCH: 1976
SEATING CAPACITY: 850
COST OF BUILDING: £185,000
ARCHITECT: MR. E.QUINN
BUILDING CONTRACTOR: D. & J. CARBERY

ASKEA (*EASCA, EASCACH* OR *EASCAIGH*; A MARSH, CONNECTED WITH *EISC*, A WATER CHANNEL; ALL DERIVED FROM THE WORD *UISCE*, MEANING WATER).

THE SITE ACQUIRED FOR THE CHURCH was part of the farm of St. Dympna's Hospital, Carlow. Askea Church was opened in a ceremony performed by Bishop Patrick Lennon. The first resident priest in Askea from 1976 was Fr. Francis MacNamara C.C. Holy Family Church served as a relief church for the Cathedral Parish, which in the previous twenty years had experienced a considerable population growth. Most Rev. Laurence Ryan constituted Askea as a new parish in 1990. It continues to be a mensal parish, like the Cathedral, with an Administrator leading the parish on behalf of the Bishop, who is technically the Parish Priest.

The church is of a unique architectural style, oval in shape. The image which inspired its design is the Old Testament moving Tent, which contained the Ark of the Covenant during the period after the Exodus, when the people of Israel wandered through the desert towards the Promised Land. Thus the roof is of a particularly unusual design.

The tabernacle is a scale replica of the building. The seating arrangement accords with the curvature of the outside walls and slopes towards the sanctuary. The resulting effect is one of greater participation in the liturgy. The baptistery and the tabernacle areas balance each other on either side of the altar area. Thus great prominence is visually given to the two Sacraments (Baptism and Eucharist), through which members are initated into the family of the Church.

The Stations of the Cross are unusual in that they are painted directly on to the brickwork. The artist was Willie Early.

Repairs were made to the roof in the late 1990s. The interior of the church has been completely refurbished during Jubilee Year 2000.

Holy Family Church, Askea.

Parish of Bennekerry

PARISH PRIEST IN THE YEAR 2000
V. REV. PATRICK DALY P.P.

CATHOLIC POPULATION: 1,300

St. Mary's Church, Bennekerry

> DATE OF CHURCH: C. 1860
> STYLE: GOTHIC
> BUILDING PASTOR: FR. JOSEPH MURRAY P.P.

BENNEKERRY (*BEANN NA GCAORACH*, PEAK OF THE SHEEP).

BENNEKERRY was part of the parish of Tinryland until 1976. Townland names in the parish such as Ballinakill, Chapelstown and Friarstown point to early chapels in the area. An old thatched church in the townland of Bennekerry, dated 1700, was used prior to St. Mary's. The granite stone for the present building came from the quarry at Graigalug. The Blessed Sacrament was first reserved in St. Mary's c. 1930.

The burial ground at the earlier church was used until 1976. Buried here is Fr. John O'Neill who, in 1798, pleaded with the local rebels not to enter Carlow, where 640 men were killed.

The internationally acclaimed artist, Frank O'Meara (1853-1888), of Dublin St., Carlow, is buried in the family tomb at Bennekerry.

The nearby dolmen at Kernanstown is one of the finest in Ireland.

The church was decorated in the early 1900s with four attractive stained glass windows in the 18th century style and eight other panels in a later style. Renovations to the church took place in 1977 when Fr. Gerard Doyle was P.P. They included the addition of a new sacristy at the church entrance and the re-ordering of the sanctuary. J. Kenneth O'Brien was the architect. Artists involved were Michael Biggs (sanctuary stonework) and Patrick McElroy (metal sanctuary furnishings). A Marian statue by Fr Henry Flanagan OP was added in 1990.

Frank O'Meara (1853 - 1888), impressionist artist

St. Mary's Church, Bennekerry

15

Parish of Arles

The Grace mausoleum, built 1818

Sacred Heart Church, Arles

DATE OF CHURCH: 1868
ARCHITECT: PUGIN AND ASHLIN
STYLE: NEO-GOTHIC
COST: £3,000

ARLES (*ÁRD GLAS*, THE VERDANT HILL,
OR *ÁRD LIOS*, THE HILL FORT).

THE ANCIENT NAME OF THIS PARISH WAS KILLABBAN, after St Abban, who built a monastery here c. 650. The parish's present name came about with the building of the parish church at Arles. The earliest chapel on this site appears to have been built in 1686. An inscribed stone in the wall of the present church records the building of this old chapel in the 1680s. This church was cruciform and thatched. In 1795 this structure was replaced by another church, which, in turn, was replaced by the present beautiful church in 1868. The present church is a most impressive structure, whose height is accentuated by its elevated site. It is lavishly built, in cut limestone, which was quarried locally. The church was constructed by local tradesmen, stone cutters and masons.

Half of the cost of the 1868 Church was contributed by the Grace family of Gracefield. The Grace Mausoleum in the adjoining cemetery was built in 1818 and replaced one built in 1687. The Grace family can trace their lineage back to Raymond Fitzwilliam, who accompanied Strongbow to Ireland.

The church was re-roofed and re-furbished in 1965 under Architect Michael Crowe and builder Michael Regan at a cost of £16,500. In 1992 the Sanctuary area was re-ordered, and the gallery and porch area were renewed. New heating and amplification was installed, as was a new Blessed Sacrament room.

Sacred Heart, Arles

The Marian Shrine in the grounds of the church was erected in memory of Fr. Donal Deady, former curate of Arles, who died on 8th Dec. 1986 in a traffic accident near Nairobi, Kenya, where he had completed two years of mission work.

John Duffy

St. Anne's Church, Ballylinan

> DATE OF CHURCH: 1969
> ARCHITECT: MR. MICHAEL CROWE
> BUILDING CONSTRUCTOR: MICHAEL
> REGAN, GRAIGUECULLEN
> COST: £23,000
> SEATING CAPACITY: 410

BALLYLINAN (*BAILE UÍ LAIGHEANÁIN*)

St. Abban's, Killeen

CLOSE TO THE VILLAGE are the ruins of an ancient church. In June 1786, in an adjoining field, some workers dug up an earthen urn which contained silver coins minted between A.D. 862 and A.D.870. The inscription on one showed it to be of the O'Mores of Leix. On the reverse was inscribed "Dúnagh-magh-Riada", i.e. Dunamase. Others belonged to the O'Conors Faly. Some of these coins are now preserved in Trinity College, Dublin.

The old church had fallen into disrepair, and on the 29th June 1969 the new church was opened and blessed by Dr. Patrick Lennon. The site was donated by Mrs Bridie Maher of Rahin, Ballylinan. The church is hexagonal in shape, supported on steel, with cavity brick walls. The roof is of aluminium alloy, and mineral felt, with the ceiling and wall panelling constructed of parana pine. In 1989, the roof was re-felted at a cost of £17,000.

Elements retained from the previous church are: the altar and tabernacle, the Stations, the statue of St. Anne, the Baptismal font and the bell.

St Abban's Church, Killeen

> DATE OF CHURCH: C. 1850
> SEATING CAPACITY: 250

THERE ARE MORE THAN EIGHTY PLACES CALLED *KILLEEN* IN IRELAND. IN BY FAR THE GREATEST NUMBER OF CASES THE NAME IS *CILLÍN* (KILLEEN), LITTLE CHURCH; BUT IN A FEW IT IS *COILLÍN*, (CULLEEN), LITTLE WOOD. KILLABBAN, WITH ITS ANCIENT MONASTIC RUINS, IS ONLY A MILE FROM KILLEEN.

THE CHURCH is of rectangular construction built of stone. The tower was a later addition. A notable feature is the beautiful stained glass window of the Crucifixion. In 1972 the church was re-latted, slated, and plastered. The Sanctuary was re-ordered and new seating installed. Renovations were also undertaken in 1978 under Architect Michael Crowe and builder Michael Regan.

St. Anne's, Ballylinan

17

John Duffy

Parish of Doonane

PARISH PRIEST IN THE YEAR 2000
V. REV. DENIS MURPHY P.P.

CATHOLIC POPULATION: 800

DOONANE (*DÚNÁN*, THE LITTLE FORT, REFERRING TO THE ANCIENT DWELLING OF KINGS AND CHIEFS. A DÚN USUALLY CONSISTED OF A HIGH CONTROL MOUND, FLAT ON TOP, SURROUNDED BY LESSER STRUCTURES).

St. Abban's Church, Doonane

THIS PARISH consists of portions of the parishes of Rathaspick and Killabban. It is relatively new (end of 1700's) and is not mentioned in the registry of 1704, the returns of 1731 and 1766, nor in Dean Skelton's list of parishes. In Rathaspick, in 1731, there was one mass-house, one priest, and one school master.

The area once supported a large anthracite industry – the seam extends from near Timahoe to the River Barrow and southwards almost to the River Nore. The Laois portion extends 3 miles × 2 miles. In 1836, 64 pits employed 700 men producing an annual output valued at £78,000.

The church is a cruciform, stone structure. The date of the building is uncertain.

The church possesses a tall silver chalice, dated 1712. Some work was conducted on the chapel in the nineteenth century by the Browne family, Farnans.

Two tablets were erected to former pastors: Rev. James Kavanagh, P.P. (died 1876), and Rev. Eugene Kelly, P.P. (died 1859), who served for 31 years in Doonane and Mayo.

St. Abban's Church, Doonane

John Duffy

Church of the Blessed Virgin Mary, Mayo

MAYO IS ALSO A CRUCIFORM CHURCH, built of stone, in the year 1826. This church has three galleries. An extensive cemetery is adjacent to the church.

The parish of Mayo and Doonane was the birthplace about 1783 of a future bishop of the diocese of Kildare and Leighlin. He was Bishop Francis Haly, nominated in late December 1837. His episcopate lasted until 1855. In 1847, Bishop Haly sanctioned the purchase of Knockbeg by Carlow College and for the period 1848-1892, Knockbeg served as a Preparatory School for the Lay College Department in St. Patrick's, Carlow College.

Right Rev. Francis Haly D. D., Bishop of Kildare and Leighlin (1857 - 1855)

Parish of Graiguecullen and Killeshin

PARISH PERSONNEL IN THE YEAR 2000
V. REV. JOHN FINGLETON P.P.
REV. THOMAS LITTLE C.C.
SR. NANCY McLOUGHLIN, R.S.M.

CATHOLIC POPULATION: 3,750

St. Clare's, Graiguecullen

GRAIGUECULLEN (*GRÁIG*, A HAMLET, VILLAGE).
IN 1909 FR. HUGH CULLEN WAS APPOINTED PARISH PRIEST OF
CARLOW-GRAIGUE AND TO PERPETUATE HIS MEMORY THE
NAME CARLOW-GRAIGUE WAS CHANGED TO GRAIGUECULLEN.

ST. FIACC (BORN 437), founder of the monastery at nearby Sleaty, was appointed by St. Patrick as the first Bishop in Leinster. The 19th century Church for Carlow-Graigue was where St. Fiacc's Hall now stands.

The Gothic Protestant Church of St. Anne on the Athy Road, Carlow was built to celebrate the victory of Colonel Henry Bruen in the 1841 election to Westminster. In 1893, Mother Seraphine Bowe and her four companions arrived at Carlow-Graigue, and began to collect money for a new convent and church. The Poor Clare Monastery was founded on its present site in 1899. In 1926, St. Anne's was purchased from Mr. Bruen of Oak Park at a nominal price. Fr. Michael Bolger, who succeeded in 1917, undertook to transfer the church across the river. The architects for the project were Messrs Foley & Sullivan.

The foundation stone was laid on 7th June 1928, and in October of the following year, the centenary of Catholic Emancipation, the church was opened and dedicated by Bishop Matthew Cullen. It stands today beside the Poor Clare Monastery, splendidly rebuilt although the steeple was not re-erected. Four parish priests were re-interred in the grounds of St. Clare's Church.

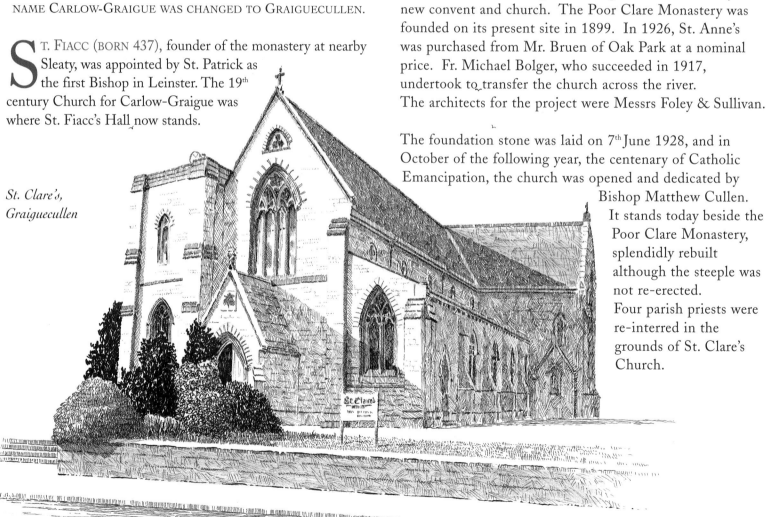

St. Clare's, Graiguecullen

Holy Cross Church, Killeshin

KILLESHIN (*CILL*, CHURCH; *OSSIAN*,
A BARD AND SON OF FIN MAC CUMHAIL).
THE DISTRICT WAS ALSO KNOWN AS GLEANN UISEAN.

AT THE BEGINNING OF THE 6TH CENTURY a monastery was founded here by St. Diarmaid. In 1041 the monastery was plundered and destroyed. The earliest of the existing remains come from a period shortly after this date. The Romanesque doorway is the most striking feature of those remains.

The founder of Holy Cross Church was Fr. Michael McDonald. Thomas Cobden was the architect. On the 6th May, 1819, the foundation stone was laid. In 1822, High Mass was celebrated there with a sermon preached by Bishop James Doyle. The church was renovated in 1966.

On an elevated site, the church of the Holy Cross is a large barn-style, stone-built structure with Gothic windows (six per side). The front elevation has a tower bearing four pinnacles, while each of the four corners carries projecting turrets. The front has three granite doorways, the only one functioning as an entrance being the central one in the tower.

The Gothic windows on the front have red-brick edging.

Romanesque Doorway, Killeshin

In the cemetery is a fine monument by Weckbecker marking the grave of Fr. Hugh Cullen, who died on 9 Aug. 1917. Interred beside him are the remains of Monsignor Patrick J. Brophy (1919-1998), who was parish priest 1976-1989. He was also parish priest of Kilcock 1974-1976, and President of Carlow College 1970-1974.

Holy Cross Church, Killeshin

John Duffy

Parish of Tinryland

PARISH PRIEST IN THE YEAR 2000
V. REV. PETER DUNNE P.P.

CATHOLIC POPULATION: 1,600

St. Joseph's Church, Tinryland

DATE OF CHURCH: 1819
BUILDING PASTOR: FR. MATTHEW MALONE
STYLE OF CHURCH: CRUCIFORM.

TINRYLAND (*TIGH AN RAOIREANN*; HOUSE OF RAOIRE; A VERY ANCIENT NAME OF A ROYAL RESIDENCE).

J.K.L. (BISHOP JAMES DOYLE) was Bishop-Elect of the diocese when he consecrated the New Church at Tinryland.

Fr. Thomas Tyrrell P.P. , Tinryland (1823-1846) played a very active role in Co. Carlow elections of M.P.'s in the 1840's to the extent of erecting in Tinryland church a 'crib' to accommodate "the black sheep who voted Tory".

A stained glass window in the church commemorates Thomas Keogh, his wife Alice, and Lt. Col. Myles Keogh, from Orchard, Leighlinbridge.

St. Joseph's Church, Tinryland

An archaeological find in Linkardstown in the 1940s proved to indicate a stone burial plot from the period 2,500-2,000 B.C. Hence such burial places are known as Linkardstown-type burials.

Church alterations took place in 1974 under architects Tyndall, Hogan & Hurley, Dublin; building contractors were the Carbery firm of Carlow. The three galleries with their stairs of stone were taken down. A new Sanctuary area was constructed and a new altar and Baptismal font of Wicklow granite installed.

Monument to Fr. Cullen erected by parishioners

Mr. Paddy Dowling, native of Linkardstown, passed away in Jubilee year 2000. He was chosen as "Carlowman of the Century" by the Old Carlow Society for his pioneering work in bringing electricity to rural Ireland in the 1940's. Tinryland parish was one of the first rural parishes in Ireland to be electrified and Tinryland church was the first rural church in Ireland to use electric lighting.

Tullow Deanery

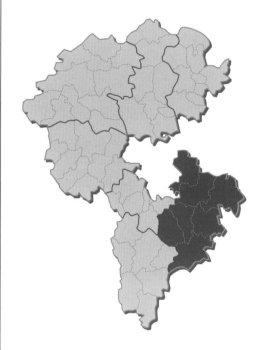

Parishes

TULLOW	24, 25
BALLON	26, 27
CLONEGAL	28, 29
CLONMORE	30, 31
RATHVILLY	32, 33, 34
BALTINGLASS	36, 37
HACKETSTOWN	38, 39, 40

Specially Featured

St. Patrick's Missionary Society   35

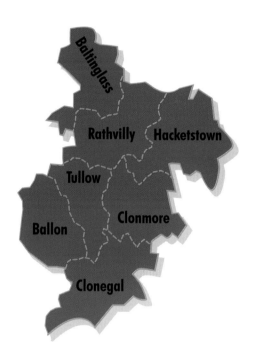

Parish of Tullow

CLERGY IN THE PARISH IN THE YEAR 2000
RT. REV. MGR. BRENDAN BYRNE P.P., V.G.
REV. WILLIAM BYRNE C.C.
REV. RORY NOLAN, SCHOOL CHAPLAIN

CATHOLIC POPULATION: 3,500

Holy Rosary, Tullow

DATE OF CHURCH: 1805
ORIGINAL STYLE: CRUCIFORM
NEW STYLE: SQUARE

TULLOW (*TULLOWPHELIM*) CONTRACTED FROM
TULLOW-OFFELIMY, THE TULACH, OR HILL OF FELIMY,
SON OF A 4TH CENTURY KING OF LEINSTER.

THE PLACE was also called Tulach Fortchern, after St. Fortchern who established schools at Killoughternane and Tullow. His pupil, St. Finian of Myshall, founded Munny, Aghowle and Clonard monasteries.

Bishop Daniel Delany, (1788–1814) founded the present church having obtained a lease from Mr. Doyne, the local landlord. As Bishop, Dr. Delany resided in Tullow. The Rebellion of 1798 caused much turbulence in the Diocese and particularly in the Tullow area. On the 2nd July, 1798, Fr. John Murphy, the Wexford rebel leader, and his companion James Gallagher were arrested near Tullow and executed in the town.

Bishop Daniel Delany

Originally the church title was The Nativity of the Blessed Virgin Mary. The tower and steeple were added in 1833. In 1872 the foundation stone was laid for the convent chapel and while it was being built, the parish church was redecorated. In 1875, Cardinal Paul Cullen rededicated the church to Our Lady of the Rosary.

Entrance to Penal Day Church, Mill St. Tullow

In 1941, Fr. James Foynes raised £10,000 to extend the church with two side aisles. These were opened in a ceremony performed by Bishop Thomas Keogh in October 1942. The architect was Mr. C.B. Powell and the builder was Mr. Thomas Flynn.

In the 1970's the sanctuary was re-ordered under the direction of architect Richard Hurley. Fr. Edward Dowling was Administrator at the time. In 1987 Fr. Peter Dunne Adm. initiated a major renovation and re-roofing and the church was rededicated in March 1990 by Bishop Laurence Ryan. The architect was Mr Patrick Campbell and the builder Mr. James Bolger.

Holy Rosary, Tullow

To mark Jubilee Year 2000 and the tenth anniversary of the renovation of the church, a new oak altar, ambo and chair were installed. The altar was blessed by Bishop Ryan in June 2000.

*Immaculate Conception,
Ardattin*

Immaculate Conception, Ardattin

DATE OF CHURCH: 1956
STYLE: ROMANESQUE
ARCHITECT: CHARLES POWELL
BUILDERS: D. & J. CARBERY, ATHY
BUILDING PASTOR: FR. JAMES DOYLE ADM.
COST: £24,500

ARDATTIN (*ARD AITINN*; HILL OF THE FURZE)

THE CHAPEL OF ST. PATRICK in Ardattin was closed in 1955 and converted into a community hall. In April 1954, the first sod was turned on a site for a new church by Bishop Thomas Keogh D.D. The site was donated by Mr Matthew Murphy of Ardoyne, Tullow.

A new marble altar and ambo were installed to mark Jubilee 2000 at a cost of £10,577.

St. John the Baptist, Grange

DATE OF CHURCH: 1822
STYLE: BARN-TYPE, RECTANGULAR
RENOVATION PASTOR: FR. PATRICK KEHOE
COST: £100; RENOVATION £80,000

GRANGE (*GRÁINSEACH*, A MONASTIC GRANARY.
IRISH WORD BORROWED FROM LATIN "GRANARIA").

IN 1148 the Cistercians founded Baltinglass Abbey. The estate headquarters in Baltinglass was known as the Abbey Demesne, and outfarms were known as 'Granges'.

The Knights Hospitaller of St. John of Jerusalem staffed the churches of Killerig and Friarstown from the end of the 12th century.

The site for the present church was secured in 1821, and a thatched church 57' x 25' was constructed.

In 1983, in a ceremony performed by the Bishop Patrick Lennon, Grange church was re-dedicated to St. John the Baptist.

Its most remembered pastor was Father John Patrick Clancy whose initials 'J.P.C.' are carved above the entrance door of the church. Fr. Clancy was born near Wexford c. 1770 and in 1811 joined the newly formed Patrician Brothers in Tullow, taking the name Brother Patrick. He combined chaplaincy to the Brothers with pastoral work at Grange.

*St. John
the Baptist, Grange*

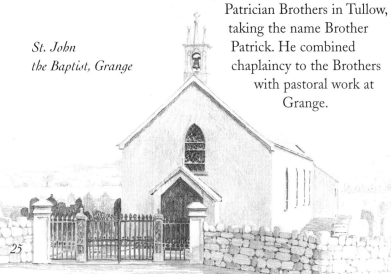

Parish of Ballon and Rathoe

St. Patrick's Church, Rathoe

> DATE OF CHURCH: 1887
> ARCHITECT: WILLIAM HAGUE
> BUILDER: CARBERY, ATHY
> STYLE: GOTHIC, STONE

RATHOE (*RATH - TUAITH*, NORTH RATH OR FORT).

THE CHURCH SITE was purchased by Bishop Daniel Delany of Tullow in the early 1800's, and the present church was built at the rear of an earlier humble structure that had existed for 100 years. Preparatory work was done by Rev. W. Kinsella P.P. and his successor, Rev. John Kehoe P.P. Fr. Kinsella had left £500 in his will towards the project and the total cost was over £3,000.

A bottle containing a Latin inscription was embedded in the new Church, and it read: "On 17th May 1885 Leo XIII being Pope over the whole church. Bishop James Walsh laid the foundation stone of the church at Rathoe. Fr. Patrick F. Nolan P.P. of Ballon & Rathoe". By 1889, Fr. Nolan was fundraising to pay for furnishings. In September of that year a huge bazaar was held in Rathoe.

An ancient Baptismal font, octagonal in shape and pierced in the centre, was transferred from the ruins of Templepeter church to St. Patrick's for the centenary in 1990. A beautiful stained glass window by Early's Studio, Dublin, overlooks the High Altar. This was erected in the 1930's. The panels depict the Annunciation, the Crucifixion and the Resurrection.

Plans were made for major renovations of the church for the year 2001.

St. Patrick's Church, Rathoe

The nearby area of Kellistown (*Cill Osnadh*, church of St. Osnadh) was an important site in the early Irish Church.

JOHN DUFFY

SS. Peter & Paul, Ballon

BALLON (BALANNA) DERIVES ITS NAME FROM THE *UÍ BALLÁIN*, A TRIBE OF THE FOTHARTA.

Ballykealy House, Patrician novitiate 1958-1984

BALLON HILL, the predominant physical feature of the area, was used extensively in Pagan times as a place of burial. In June 1853, Mr. J. Richardson Smith, brother-in-law to Mr. Lecky of Ballykealy House, conducted a dig on the hill. He discovered a unique collection of vessels.

The original rectangular church was built in stages from 1714 to 1731 during Penal Times and was thatched; it consisted of the present two side-aisles. The walls in the present church are built with granite from Ballon Hill. This stone is very hard and has a green tint. Now cruciform, the church's long aisle was built by Rev. John Kehoe P.P., in the 1870's. He also roofed the church with slates. A bust of Fr. Kehoe is placed in the main aisle.

In October 1901 the new High Altar was consecrated by Bishop Patrick Foley in memory of Fr. P.F. Nolan P.P. Atop the four gables are four granite crosses, each one a different style. Internal refurbishing took place 1977-1978, with further renovations in 1996-1997.

There is a plaque in the northern transept to Fr. James Conran P.P. 1802-1825. He was Vicar Capitular of the Diocese when Dr. Doyle was appointed Bishop in 1819.

The noted historian, William Edward Hartpole Lecky (1838-1903) was a connection of the Leckys, Ballykealy House, Ballon. Ballykealy House served as Novitiate for the Patrician Brothers from 1958 to 1984.

In 1953, Cardinal Francis Spellman, Archbishop of New York, visited Ballon while in the area en route to Kildavin.

SS. Peter & Paul, Ballon

John Duffy

Parish of Clonegal

PARISH PRIEST IN THE YEAR 2000
V. REV. JOSEPH FLEMING P.P.

CATHOLIC POPULATION: 1,700

St. Brigid's Church, Clonegal

DATE OF CHURCH: 1824
BUILDERS: HICKEYS, KILCARRY
BUILDING PASTOR: FR. MARTIN DOYLE P.P.
(1818-1827)
STYLE: BARN-TYPE

CLONEGAL (*CLUAIN NA NGALL*,
MEADOW OF THE GALLS OR FOREIGNERS).

THE ANCIENT PARISH NAME was Barragh and Moyacomb. The church of *Barragh* was destroyed in 1650 by Cromwell's soldiers. A Patron Day took place here until 1798. The holy well was restored for Jubilee 2000. Moyacomb is from Magh da chon, and refers to the plain of the two hounds, the ancestral patrimony of O'Neill of Leinster.

Clonegal, on the river Derry, was where the coach roads from the midlands, Kildare and Dublin converged.

The present church is a large structure and was constructed around the previous thatched chapel then in use. Stone for the church came from a quarry in Monaughrim. The ceiling has beautiful work by Italian artisans.

St. Brigid's Church, Clonegal

The bell tower is pointed with four miniature spires. The most important feature of the Sanctuary area is the paired Corinthian columns, flanked by pilasters and surmounted by an open pediment.

In the year 2000, a Jubilee Cross (by Brendan Dunbar of Courtown) was erected in the adjoining graveyard.

St. Laserian's Church, Kildavin

John Duffy

St. Laserian's Church, Kildavin

DATE OF CHURCH: 1830
STYLE: BARN-TYPE
BUILDING PASTOR: FR. PATRICK DOLAN P.P

KILDAVIN (*CILL DAMHÁIN,* CHURCH OF ST. DUBHAN, THE BLACK-HEADED ONE)

AN ANCIENT RELIGIOUS SETTLEMENT existed here on the banks of the River Slaney and from this, the place derives its name. St Abban is thought to have built a cell in this area. In the 5th - 6th century St. Dubhan of Rath Dubhain flourished. His feast occurs on 11th February.

St. Laserian's is a small structure built of stone. The shaft in the bell tower bears the date 1844 . For Jubilee Year 2000 a cross by Patsy Slye of Kilmyshal was erected in the grounds.

On 31st October 1953, Cardinal Francis Spellman (1889-1967), Archbishop of New York, visited Kildavin Cemetery.
The Cardinal's grandmother, Ellen Kehoe (1834-1914), was born at Sherwood, Kilbride. She emigrated to America.
The Cardinal donated Kildavin Hall to the village, in her memory. Spellman G.A.A. Park, Kildavin, was opened on October 11th 1970.

In the 1970's both churches in the parish were re-ordered. [Fr. Gerard O'Mahony P.P. ; Michael Crowe, Architect; Michael Regan, Builder; Total cost: £59,000]

Cardinal Francis Spellman

29

Parish of Clonmore

CLERGY IN THE PARISH IN THE YEAR 2000
V. REV. CHARLES BYRNE P.P.
REV. VINCENT MCDONALD C.S.SP., C.C.

CATHOLIC POPULATION: 1,600

Aghowle Monastery, founded by Finian in the 6th century

Our Lady of the Wayside Church, Clonmore

> DATE OF CHURCH: 1968
> BUILDING PASTOR: FR. TOM MCDONALD P.P.
> ARCHITECT: N.E. HARVEY

CLONMORE (*CLUAIN MÓR*, BIG MEADOW), ALSO *CLUAIN-MÓR-MAEDHOC*, REFERRING TO ST. MAEDHOC, FOUNDER OF A MONASTERY HERE IN THE 6TH CENTURY.

FROM THE EARLIEST TIMES, Clonmore was a centre of sanctity and learning, with many saints associated with its monastery. St. Finian founded a monastery at Aghold early in the 6th century (*Achadh abhla*, field of apples).

Clonmore Castle is thought to have been built c. 1180 by DeLacy, while tradition associated it with the Hackett family from whom Hacketstown is named.

The site for the modern church of Our Lady of the Wayside was donated by Billy Byrne. It is a pre-cast structure, by Banagher Concrete Co., and was assembled on site. The foundation stone states that it was blessed and laid by Bishop Patrick Lennon.

In Jubilee Year 2000, Fr. William Dempsey of Daingean, Co. Offaly published *A Light from the Grave*, which traces the life of Fr. Andrew Mullen, who served in Clonmore parish at the beginning of the 19th century. This priest gave all he had to the poor and had a reputation for being a healer of the sick. Fr. Andrew Mullen died in 1818, aged 27 and was buried beside the old church in Clonmore. Five weeks later, his friends and relations from Daingean exhumed his body and brought it to Co. Offaly, where the priest was re-interred in Killaderry cemetery.

Buried in the old graveyard beside St. Bridget's church is Rev. Felix Nolan (d. 1774) who served the parish for more than 50 years.

Our Lady of the Wayside Church, Clonmore

John Duffy

St. Mary's Church, Ballyconnell

DATE OF CHURCH: 1833
BUILDING PASTOR: FR. PHILIP HEALY P.P.

BALLYCONNELL (*BAILE UÍ CHONAILL*; TOWN OF CONAL).

THE SITE FOR THIS CHURCH was given by Mr. Patrick Hughes. He was granted permission to do so by Lord Earl Fitzwilliam, landlord of Coolattin Estate. The site was chosen because of its proximity to the school which had been built in 1827.

The church is a large structure solidly constructed of local granite using marl mixed with lime. The oak timber used came from Coolattin Estate. The carpenter was Patrick Murphy and the masons were Hanley Bros. of Knockballystine.

A gallery was added later, and two stained-glass windows were donated by Johanna Shepard, Ballyconnell. The church has a chalice from the old Knockballystine chapel. The altar was erected in memory of Fr. John Boland, P.P. 1866-1886.

St. Mary's Church, Ballyconnell

St. Finian's Church, Kilquiggan

St. Finian's Church, Kilquiggan

DATE OF CHURCH: 1890
BUILDING PASTOR:FR. WILLIAM BYRNE P.P.

KILQUIGGAN (*CILL CHOMHGAFIN*).

ST. FIACC was appointed first Bishop of Leinster by St. Patrick. He founded a monastery between Clonmore and Aghold at a place named Domnach Fiacc.

The present Kilquiggan church stands on a site given by Mr. Wall, a member of the Church of Ireland. The church is constructed of granite from a quarry at Killabeg. The stone was cut by Connolly Bros., Kilquiggan. The Hanley brothers of Knockballystine were the masons employed.

The local Coolattin Estate, awned by the Fitzwilliam family, extended from Shillelagh to Bray, and in 1838 was the largest estate in Co. Wicklow comprising over 75,000 acres. Coolattin oak is world renowned.

Lady Alice Mary Wentworth Fitzwilliam, sister of the landlord of Coolattin Estate, converted to Catholicism. After her wedding she donated her wedding gown to be made into vestments for the altar servers. Hers was the first burial in the present church grounds.

Parish of Rathvilly

CLERGY IN THE PARISH IN THE YEAR 2000
V. REV. EDWARD FLOOD P.P.
V. REV. DERMOT MCDERMOT P.E., C.C.

CATHOLIC POPULATION: 2,200

St. Patrick's Church, Rathvilly

DATE OF CHURCH: 1887
STYLE: GOTHIC
ARCHITECT: WILLIAM HAGUE
BUILDER: JOHN HARRIS, MONASTEREVIN
BUILDING PASTOR: FR. PATRICK C. NOLAN P.P.

RATHVILLY (RATH-BHILE; THE FORT OF THE GREAT TREE).

BILE referred to a large tree held in veneration, usually where chiefs were inaugurated, or games celebrated. A great insult was for one tribe to cut down the ceremonial tree of another. Such a tree must have existed in Rathvilly.

The Rath is thought to have formed a link in a series of earthen forts which included Eagle Hill, Clonmore, Tullow and Castlemore.

Architect's drawing showing steeple intended for St. Patrick's

Crimthann, who became King of Leinster in 443, is said to have been baptised by St. Patrick with his family at Rathvilly in 450.

Building began on the present church in 1883. Stone came from granite quarries in the vicinity. The church is described in *The Nation* as "comprising nave, aisles, chancel, two side chapels, large sacristies, with parochial room over same, and tower and porch to the north and south aisles respectively. The clear length inside is 127ft., width 28ft., chancel 28ft. x 27ft, and the height of the nave and chancel 60ft. to ridge. The aisles are divided from the nave by five bays of granite moulded arches".

Fr. Patrick C. Nolan, P.P. 1855-1885, died before the church was completed. It opened in 1887 when Fr. John Phelan was P.P. Fr. Bernard Ryan P.P. (1983-1993) had the Church interior re-ordered in 1988. A Prayer Room was provided close to the Pulpit.

St. Patrick's Church, Rathvilly

St. Brigid's Church, Talbotstown

> DATE OF CHURCH: 1842
> STYLE: BARN-TYPE
> BUILDING PASTOR: FR. JOHN GAHAN P.P.

THIS AREA IS REFERRED TO IN 1500 AS 'TALBOTISTON'
(KILDARE RENTAL JRSAI VII, 123).
THE NAME OF TALBOTSTOWN DERIVES FROM THE TALBOT
FAMILY AND DATES FROM THE 13TH CENTURY.

THE CHURCH OF ST BRIGID is a substantial structure built of granite, with a front of fine-cut blocks featuring six pillars. Three doorways allow access, two to the nave and the central one to the organ gallery. The porch has rounded stone arches, a feature repeated in the side-windows and the pillar-supported arch over the old altar.

A modern altar has been positioned facing the people. The organ came from the Presentation Convent, Carlow, in the early 1990's. The present church replaced the church of St. Brigid at Englishtown. The bell of the old church was installed in Talbotstown. The Holy Water Font from the old church went to St. Joseph's in Baltinglass.

Internally, the striking features are the high walls of exposed stone which support a beautiful ceiling painted by Grispini, an Italian artist who also worked on Humewood Castle, Kiltegan.

The stonework was pointed in 1974 and following the storm of 1997 new windows were installed. The church has never had stained-glass windows.

The locality is dominated by Humewood Estate. The Wicklow rebel Michael Dwyer of Imaal was arrested near Humewood Estate in 1803.

Michael Dwyer (1772-1825)

St. Brigid's Church, Talbotstown

John Duffy

John Duffy

Church of the Assumption, Tynock

DATE OF CHURCH: 1829
STYLE: CRUCIFORM
BUILDING PASTOR: FR. PATRICK MOORE P.P.

TYNOCK (*TIG AN CNOIC*; HOUSE OF THE HILL).

THE HILL IN QUESTION has a spectacular view of the Wicklow Mountains. The church is built of local granite. Prior to this church, the area was served by a chapel in Tinneclash. The pre-1829 church became a school house.

Nearby is the village of Kiltegan (deriving from St. Tegan, a companion of St. Fiacc of Clonmore). His church has disappeared.

The choir gallery was removed and the altar moved forward in recent times. The old parochial house and oratory at Kiltegan were sold in 1982 and a new bungalow and oratory (St. Tegan's) were constructed.

ST. PATRICK'S MISSIONARY SOCIETY (KILTEGAN FATHERS)

WHILE WORKING IN NIGERIA IN 1921, a young Fr Patrick Joseph Whitney, native of Breenletter, Co. Roscommon, devised a scheme to establish a Society similar to the Maynooth Mission to China. He had been Bishop Shanahan's first volunteer to Africa, in 1920. St. Patrick's Missionary Society was founded in 1932 with Fr. Pat as the first Superior General. John Hughes (1886-1934), of Kilkeel, Co. Down, who had worked as a young man in the grocery trade in Liverpool and, in time, had his own business comprising sixty grocery shops in and around Liverpool, offered High Park, Kiltegan, to the proposed Missionary Society at a bargain price. He soon realised that Fr. Whitney had no money and proceeded to make a gift to the Society, granting them, at first, the house with walled garden and a few fields. He knew their thoughts were on Africa rather than farming and decided to release the land gradually to them.

He had an arch made for the gate with the new house-name, Our Lady of Africa, worked into it. Six months after its foundation, ten young men arrived in Kiltegan to join the new Missionary Society. The Society's first priests arrived in Nigeria in 1939 and another sixty Kiltegan missionaries followed them in the next decade. The number of missionary vocations was so great that in the late 1950s it was decided to build a new college in Kiltegan and to expand the Society's other house of formation in Cork. To date, more than six hundred missionary priests have been ordained for the Society an students from Africa and, hopefully, in the near future from South America, are preparing to become missionary priests of the Society founded seventy years ago by Fr. Pat Whitney in West Wicklow. The Society, today, continues its missionary ministry in Nigeria, Kenya, Malawi, Zambia, Sudan, Rwanda, Cameroon, Zimbabwe, South Africa, Brazil and Grenada. The Superior General is Fr. Kieran Birmingham from Lusmagh, Co. Offaly.

St. Patrick's, Kiltegan, Co. Wicklow

Parish of Baltinglass

PARISH PERSONNEL IN THE YEAR 2000
V. REV. GERALD DOYLE P.P.
REV. PADRAIG SHELLEY C.C.
SR. BRIGID MORGAN RSM

CATHOLIC POPULATION: 2,900

St. Joseph's Church, Baltinglass

DATE OF CHURCH: C. 1855
BUILDING PASTOR: FR. DANIEL LALOR P.P.

Cistercian Abbey, Baltinglass, founded in 1148

BALTINGLASS (*BEALACH CHONGLAIS*;
THE WAY OR ROAD OF CUGLAS). CU-GLAS WAS MASTER OF
HOUNDS FOR THE KING OF IRELAND.

THE CISTERCIANS established an Abbey on the banks of the River Slaney at Baltinglass in 1148, on a site granted by Diarmaid Mac Murchadha. It was a daughter house of Mellifont, Co. Louth.

The church of St. Joseph was built during the pastorate of Fr. Daniel Lalor, P.P. (1831-1871) and Curacy of Fr. John Nolan. The interior work was done by Dr. Denis Kane, P.P. 1871-1883.

A tower was erected in the adjoining cemetery to serve as belfry. A statute was enacted in the reign of George III that no Roman Catholic chapel could have a steeple or a bell; hence the appearance of bells mounted separately from their churches.

St. Joseph's Church, Baltinglass

St. Mary's Church, Stratford-on-Slaney

DATE OF CHURCH: c. 1840
RENOVATION ARCHITECT: PAUL O'DALY

STRATFORD-ON-SLANEY (*ÁTH NA SRÁIDE*)

THE VILLAGE OF STRATFORD takes its name from the Stratford family. The Stratfords came to Ireland in the 17th century and purchased Belan near Moone, Co. Kildare. The Stratford estates in seven counties amounted to 28,000 acres. The village dates from c. 1783.

The first outbreak of the 1798 rebellion in Co. Wicklow occurred on 24th May when an attack on Stratford-on-Slaney failed and the rebels were put to flight along the Baltinglass road with heavy losses.

St. Mary's is a small cruciform structure built c. 1840. It replaced a little chapel that had been built in the 1780's. It was renovated in 1981 in the pastorate of Fr. Thomas F. Brophy.

St. Mary's Church, Stratford-on-Slaney

St. Oliver's Church, Grangecon

St. Oliver's Church, Grangecon

DATE OF CHURCH: 1978
ARCHITECT: PAUL O'DALY
BUILDER: P. FURLONG, BUNCLODY
SEATING: 400

GRANGECON (*GRÁINSEACH CHOINN*; GRANGE OF CONN)

THE OUTFARMS OR ABBEY DEMESNES were called granges, derived from the Latin work 'granaria', a granary. As a result, many placenames based on the word 'grange' are common within fifteen miles of Baltinglass.

An old chapel was demolished to make way for the modern church of St. Oliver Plunkett. The cost was £128,000. Tapestries were done by Michele Holler, Kilkenny, and Liturgical Elements were provided by Chris and Elizabeth Ryan, Dublin. The church was dedicated on 6th August 1978 in a ceremony performed by Bishop Patrick Lennon assisted by parish priest Fr. Thomas F. Brophy.

Parish of Hacketstown

CLERGY IN THE PARISH IN THE YEAR 2000
V. REV. PATRICK J. MCDONNELL P.P.
REV. JAMES MC CORMACK M.S.C., C.C.

CATHOLIC POPULATION: 1,700

St. Brigid's, Hacketstown

DATE OF CHURCH: 1803
STYLE: BARN-TYPE
BUILDING PASTOR: FR. JOHN BLANCHFIELD P.P.

HACKETSTOWN (RECENTLY *BAILE HAICÉID*; OLDER *BAILE AN DROICHID,* A REFERENCE TO THE BRIDGE CROSSING THE RIVER DERREEN, A TRIBUTARY OF THE SLANEY).

A CASTLE, contemporary with that of Clonmore, once stood at Hacketstown. Its site was later occupied by a barracks which, in turn, became the site of the present parish church. Clonmore castle was built c. 1180, and was the possession of the Hackett family. On 25th June, 1798, over 10,000 rebels engaged in the Battle of Hacketstown.

Stone cross used in Penal Day Church, Hacketstown

The stone-walled barracks proved impenetrable.

The present church is constructed of granite, and has a gallery at its rear. The steeple, of cut granite, was added by Fr. Patrick Morrin P.P., (1836-1855). Mounted in the church is a stone bearing a rough impression of the crucifixion. It has been dated to 1610 and belonged to the original Catholic church on the Carlow Road and the thatched chapel on the Green.

St. Brigid's, Hacketstown

John Duffy

Immaculate Conception, Knockananna

DATE OF CHURCH: 1978
ARCHITECT: PAUL O'DALY
BUILDER: P. FURLONG, BUNCLODY
BUILDING PASTOR: FR. PATRICK BOYLAN P.P.
SEATING: 400
COST: £110,000

KNOCKANANNA
(*CNOC AN EANAIGH*; HILL OF THE MARSH).

Knockananna's Old Church

Church of Our Lady, Killamoate

DATE OF CHURCH: 1850
STYLE: BARN-TYPE
BUILDING PASTOR: FR. PATRICK MORRIN P.P

KILLAMOATE (*COILL AN MHÓTA*, WOOD OF THE MOAT). THE REMAINS OF AN ANGLO-NORMAN MOUND OR MOAT EXIST ON THE EASTERN SIDE OF THE CROSSROADS AND CHURCH.

OUR LADY'S CHURCH is a spacious stone-built structure. It was built over the preceding church.

Two beautiful stained glass windows by Harry Clarke were installed in the 1920's. Six new windows, sponsored by local people, were added to complement the Clarke windows. In 1968, the church was re-roofed and renovated at a cost of £24,000.

THE OLD CHURCH IN KNOCKANANNA was built at the beginning of the 1800's. It serves the community today as "The Blanchvelle Centre".

The modern church has tapestries by Michelle Hillaire, Kilkenny. The Liturgical Elements are by Chris Ryan, Dublin. Bishop Patrick Lennon performed the opening ceremony on 1st March 1978.

The "Self-Help" organisation was begun in 1984 by Fr. Owen Lambert, C.S.Sp., and his family in Knockananna. Based on agricultural principles the organisation helps many farming communities in African Countries.

*Immaculate Conception,
Knockananna*

St. Mary's Church, Askinagap

> DATE OF CHURCH: C. 1820
> STYLE: BARN-TYPE

ASKINAGAP (*EASCA NA GCEAP. EASCA: MARSH, WET AREA; CEAP: STOCK OF A TREE*).

IN ITS HEYDAY THE NEARBY COOLE ESTATE provided much employment and "The O'Mahony" is remembered as a kind and generous landlord. In an 1876 listing of Wicklow's Landed Gentry, is "Mahony, acres 1,769; valuation £1,434".

On the wall of the church are two plaques. One is by O'Mahony in thankfulness for safe passage through the Great War and the other states the following: "To the memory of the Mulhall Family, Askinagap, all six who died on 23rd March

1867 in the great snow storm. Interred in Preban R.I.P." The family's home was engulfed in an avalanche.

About 1950 buttresses were erected to support bulging sidewalls, the church was re-roofed and a new sacristy built. Further work was done and alterations made to the sanctuary area in 1972.

Askinagap is the most easterly church in the Diocese of Kildare and Leighlin.

The O'Mahoney in typical dress, with his piper.

St. Mary's Church, Askinagap

John Duffy

BORRIS DEANERY

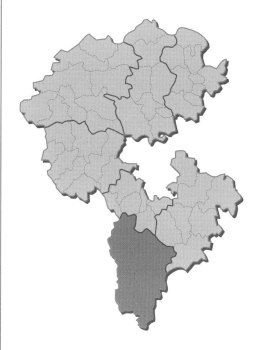

PARISHES

BORRIS	42, 43, 44
ST. MULLINS	46, 47
GRAIGNAMANAGH	48, 49
MYSHALL	50, 51
MUINE BHEAG	52, 53
PAULSTOWN	54, 55
LEIGHLIN	56, 57

SPECIALLY FEATURED

Religious Orders and Congregations	45
Leighlin Cathedral (Church of Ireland)	58

Parish of Borris

CLERGY IN THE PARISH IN THE YEAR 2000
V. REV. NICHOLAS MOORE P.P.
REV. TONY CRONIN S.P.S., C.C.

CATHOLIC POPULATION: 2,000

Borris House, home of Mc Murrough Kavanaghs

Sacred Heart, Borris

DATE OF CHURCH: 1820
BUILDING PASTOR: FR. JOHN WALSH P.P.
DATE OF ENLARGEMENT: 1896

BORRIS (*BUIRGHÉIS,* A BURGAGE OR BOROUGH).

THE KAVANAGHS OF THE BARONY OF IDRONE, Co. Carlow, were for centuries the main obstacle to English rule at the limits of the Pale. In the 1700's they possessed over 28,000 acres. By 1825 the Kavanaghs had adopted the Protestant religion.

The site for the present church was provided by the McMurrough Kavanagh family of Borris House. The church has a facade of granite decorated with limestone which incorporates a Romanesque style doorway. The stained glass window over the main altar consists of three granite-framed panels depicting the crucifixion, with the three under portions depicting Sts. Fortchern, Brigid and Fiachra.

The sanctuary was re-ordered by Fr. Peter Boylan P.P. (1956-1985). The church was re-roofed in 2000 by Fr. Nicholas Moore P.P. The architect was Eamon Hedderman, and the builder Seán Egars.

Dr. Patrick Lennon, Bishop of Kildare & Leighlin (1967-1987), was a native of Borris.

Sacred Heart, Borris

St. Patrick's, Ballymurphy

DATE OF CHURCH: 1846
BUILDING PASTOR: FR. CHRISTOPHER DOYLE P.P.

BALLYMURPHY - NAMED AFTER MATTHEW MURPHY OF CLONROCHE, A POWERFUL LANDOWNER AND BUILDER OF A CASTLE IN THE AREA IN THE MID-17TH CENTURY. THE 'RATHGERAN STONE' IN THE VICINITY IS THOUGHT TO BE VERY ANCIENT, PERHAPS AS OLD AS NEWGRANGE.

THE GRANITE STONES FOR ST. PATRICK'S are hammer-dressed. The church bell was removed and erected on the school grounds beside Borris church. A new bell, presented by Mr. Byrne (Bell founder, Dublin), native of Ballymurphy, was erected on an iron tower in 1914.

Famous natives of Ballymurphy were: Edmund Byrne of Ballybrack, Archbishop of Dublin c. 1700 and Edward Murphy of Knockmore, Bishop of Kildare & Leighlin (1715-1724) and Archbishop of Dublin (1724-1729).

Patrick and Margaret Breen, Donner Pass survivors

A new car park was added to the church in 1986. In 1987 the church was painted, re-ordered, and was given a new roof and ceiling. Eamon Hedderman was the Architect.

Patrick Breen of Barnahasken (1795-1868) was at the centre of the story of the Donner Pass in the Sierra Nevada mountains. He and his family joined others in 1846-1847 in the ill-fated passage through the snows of the Sierras in which 39 people perished. Subsequently the Breens flourished in San Juan Bautista, California.

St. Patrick's, Ballymurphy

John Duffy

St. Fortchern's Church, Rathanna

St. Fortchern's Church, Rathanna

DATE OF CHURCH: 1885
ARCHITECT: WILLIAM HAGUE
STYLE: EARLY GOTHIC
BUILDING PASTOR: FR. PATRICK CAREY P.P.
COST: £2,000

RATHANNA (*RATH AN EANAIGH,* FORT OF THE MARSH).

RATHANNA is situated at the foot of Mount Leinster. St. Fortchern established a monastery at nearby Killoughternane. He was a disciple of St. Patrick.

The site for the present church was donated by Mrs McDonald, Rathanna, and adjoined that of an earlier church, St. Anne's. Prior to that date, the people had to attend Mass in either Borris or Ballymurphy. The belfry of St. Anne's is still in use.

Mrs McDonald, Rathanna, paid for the building of the church and for the original carved altar. The top portion of the stained glass windows behind the altar depicting Our Lady and St. Anne came from the old church. On 24th May 1900, the church was dedicated, by Bishop Patrick Foley. On the 2nd June 1985, its centenary was marked with a mass celebrated by Bishop Patrick Lennon.

In 1991 the gallery was removed and internal porches constructed inside the east and west doors, and the work incorporated a lobby and reconciliation room. This work was carried out under the direction of Fr. Nicholas Moore P.P., by Murphy Bros. (contractors) to the design of architect Eamon Hedderman. The roof was cleaned, leaded, and repaired.

The churchyard contains the graves of the three members of the Shannon family, Knockroe, who died when their home was destroyed by German Bombers on New Year's Eve, 1941.

RELIGIOUS ORDERS AND CONGREGATIONS

THE MISSION of the Church in this diocese has been assisted at many stages of its history by male and female institutes of consecrated life.

In the early stages of their history Kildare and Leighlin dioceses were organised on a monastic basis. The Celtic monasteries were well represented from the 6th to the 11th centuries at

Clongowes Wood Castle

several centres: Kildare (female and male communities) under the inspiration of St. Brigid and St. Conleth; Old Leighlin with its monastery; Clonenagh (near present Mountrath) founded by St. Fintan; Killabban; Killeshin and Sleaty (both in the present parish of Graiguecullen); St. Mullins; Killashee; Killeigh and several other sites.

The Synods of Rathbrassil and Kells (in the 12th century) set up the Irish dioceses with ancient monastic centres giving their names to new dioceses. The same period saw the advent of several mendicant and other orders from Europe. Most significant were the Cistercian foundations: three in Leighlin diocese (Baltinglass, Abbeyleix and Duiske – Graignamanagh) and one in Kildare (at Monasterevin). Several parishes have long associations with other orders in the medieval period: Carlow and Monasteroris-Edenderry (Franciscans), Kildare and Leighlinbridge (Carmelites), Naas (Dominicans) and Tullow (Augustinians).

From the 16th century Reformation period to the early 19th century the presence of Religious in Kildare and Leighlin was less – though there is evidence of many friars ministering in all areas of the diocese during the Penal Law era.

The last 200 years have seen a strong increase in the foundation of Religious Houses. The majority of these have provided educational service, though some have concentrated on the care of the handicapped and the sick in hospitals and other centres.

Bishop Daniel Delany (1787-1814) founded two Congregations: Brigidine Sisters and Patrician Brothers. The Brigidines have had houses in the parishes of Tullow, Mountrath, Abbeyleix, Paulstown and Kildare while the Patricians have been based in the parishes of Tullow, Mountrath, Ballyfin, Abbeyleix, Ballon and Newbridge.

Another early 19th century foundation was that of the Jesuits at Clongowes Wood, Clane, Co. Kildare. Fr. Peter Kenney S.J.

was the first Rector from 1814. The school there has educated a long stream of distinguished Irishmen, including James Joyce. The Dominicans conduct a secondary school in Newbridge – a foundation in continuity with the medieval Naas foundation. The Carmelite community in Kildare Town can claim over 700 years of association with the parish. The Salesian Fathers have served in education since 1941 in Ballinakill.

The Oblate Fathers had a long association with Daingean, Co. Offaly. Their apostolate for a long period included an industrial school for boys. The Capuchin Franciscans have been in Carlow Town since 1977. A very notable development within the diocese was the establishment of St. Patrick's Missionary Society at Kiltegan, Co. Wicklow. The Society is administered in its worldwide apostolate from Kiltegan.

The Christian Brothers worked for over 150 years in the diocese in the following parishes: Naas, Kilcock, Monasterevin, Portarlington, Portlaoise and Carlow. Likewise the De La Salle Brothers founded and conducted schools in Bagenalstown and Kildare.

The diocese has been greatly served by numerous female Religious Congregations. Besides the work of the Brigidine Sisters, the following have worked and in most cases still work in the diocese:

- Mercy Sisters (Carlow, Graignamanagh, Leighlinbridge, Graiguecullen, Monasterevin, Rathangan and Naas).
- Presentation Sisters (Carlow, Askea, Bagenalstown, Monasterevin, Portarlington, Portlaoise, Stradbally, Mountmellick, Kilcock, Kildare and Clane).
- Sisters of St. John of God (Edenderry and Naas).
- St. Clare Sisters (Monasterevin).
- Poor Clare Sisters (Graiguecullen).
- Hospitallers of the Sacred Heart of Jesus (Carlow).
- Sisters of the Holy Family of Bordeaux (Newbridge and Portlaoise).
- Daughters of Mary and Joseph (Newbridge).
- Sisters of Charity of Jesus and Mary (Monasterevin).

The Focolare Movement (mainly with lay membership) has recently established a House at Prosperous, Co. Kildare.

Parish of St. Mullins

PARISH PRIEST IN THE YEAR 2000
V. REV. EDWARD AUGHNEY P.P.

CATHOLIC POPULATION: 1,200

St. Mullins

THE ORIGINAL NAME FOR THIS AREA WAS ROS BROC, (THE WOOD OF THE BADGER), SITUATED IN A VALLEY BY THE RIVER BARROW, IN SOUTH CARLOW.

St. Moling's Monastery, St. Mullins

ST. MOLING founded his monastery here in the early part of the 7th century. Ros Broc became Teach Moling, then Saint Mullins. St. Moling also spent some time at Glendalough and later became Bishop of Ferns. He died in 697. A man of great piety, he spent seven years labouring on a mill race which brought water to the monastery. It is about a mile in length and diverted water from the Glynn river. St. Mullins, the most notable pilgrimage site in the diocese, celebrates its Pattern Day on the Sunday after 25th July.

The Kavanaghs of Borris, who regarded St. Moling as their patron saint, presented to Trinity College, Dublin, the ancient family heirloom of the Evangelistarium of St. Moling. This manuscript collection was housed in a box made of brass encased in silver. The vellum sheets contained extracts from the Gospels and prayers for the sick, in Latin. There were also drawings of the Apostles, thought to be the work of St. Moling.

St. Mullins has long been the burial place for the Kavanaghs, Kings of Leinster, and it is said that the funeral of Art Mac Murrough in 1417 reached from New Ross to St. Mullins, a distance of about six miles.

Church of St. Moling, Glynn

DATE OF CHURCH: C. 1820
STYLE: CRUCIFORM
BUILDING PASTOR: FR. THOMAS MOORE P.P.
EXTENSION BUILDER: EDWARD CAHILL, MARLEY

GLYNN (*AN GLEANN*, A GLEN OR VALLEY).

DESCRIBED BY DR. COMERFORD as "a handsome edifice surrounded by trim and tastefully kept grounds", the church is of plastered stone. It was extended during the pastorate of Fr. Joseph Ferris P.P. (1867-1896). Fr. Joseph McDonnell P.P. re-ordered the church in 1971. The two side galleries were taken down. The bell was electrified in 1990 by John Doran, Marley. The church has in its possession a chalice dated 1684 donated by Thomas Mulcahy and wife Brigid (nee Dunne). The stone pillars and the baptismal font were carved by Cahills of Marley.

In the 1880's a school teacher at Glynn, James Murphy, wrote several books including *The Forge of Clohogue, Emmet's Day*, and *Convict No. 25*.

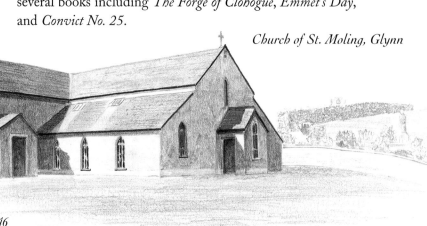

Church of St. Moling, Glynn

Church of St. Brendan, Drummond

Kavanagh ('The Cripple') M.P. 1868-1880, who sailed his yacht 'Eva' to parliamentary sessions in Westminster.

DATE OF CHURCH: 1829
BUILDING PASTOR: FR. THOMAS DOWLING P.P.
STYLE: BARN-TYPE

DRUMMOND (A CORRUPT FORM OF DRUMMIN; SAME MEANING AS DRUIM, A RIDGE OR LONG HILL).

THIS CHURCH IS A LARGE STRUCTURE built of plastered stone. An earlier structure stood on the site, which was first used as a hedge school and after 1833 as a National School. In 1975 the Church was renovated and re-dedicated under the guidance of Fr. Joseph McDonnell PP (1969-1975). Nearby in Drummond Wood was The Cripple's Cottage and a wooden jetty used as a landing stage for Arthur McMurrough

BISHOP LAURENCE RYAN was born in 1931 at Ballycrinnigan in this parish. He attended Glynn N.S., and Knockbeg and Maynooth Colleges. In 1956 he was ordained to the priesthood. For two years he pursued Doctoral studies at Maynooth. He taught in Carlow College for twenty-two years and was President there from 1974 to 1980. He was Parish Priest of Naas from 1980 to 1985 and Vicar General of Kildare and Leighlin from 1975 to 1987. He was ordained Coadjutor Bishop on 9th September 1984, and succeeded as Bishop of Kildare and Leighlin on 10th December 1987. He has been President of the Irish Commission for Justice and Peace since 1995 and was Chairman of the Jubilee 2000 Committee (1997-2000).

Church of St. Brendan, Drummond

John Duffy

Parish of Graignamanagh

CLERGY IN THE PARISH IN THE YEAR 2000
V. REV. GERALD S. BYRNE P.P.
REV. DERMOT KIELY S.P.S., C.C.

CATHOLIC POPULATION: 2,400

Duiske Abbey, Graignamanagh

DATE OF ABBEY: 1204
RESTORATION WORK: 1974-1980
RESTORATION PASTOR: FR. WILLIAM GAVIN P.P.

GRAIGNAMANAGH

(*GRAIG NA MANACH*, GRANGE OF THE MONKS).

IN ANCIENT RECORDS it is styled the Abbey of Duiske, from the confluence of the Duiske stream, the Black Water, with the River Barrow.

William Marshall, earl of Pembroke, introduced Cistercians from Stanley Abbey in Wiltshire c. 1202. It took forty years to build the Abbey and twelve years to build the church. The Abbey is identical in plan to the church of Strata Florida in Cardiganshire, and with a nave of over 200ft. was the finest Irish Cistercian monastery. The area prospered. Bog and mountain were reclaimed and a wool trade established with Italian firms who had agents in Waterford and Dublin. The river provided much fish and two monastic eel weirs still survive.

The Knight of Duiske, c. 1300

Duiske Abbey, Graignamanagh

Abbot Charles O'Kavanagh, anticipating the suppression of the monasteries by King Henry VIII, sent some of the young monks to Regensburg in Germany. From 1541 the property was held by various Butler descendants. The Abbey still has in its possession a beautiful silver chalice of Lady Anna Butler, dated 1636. Despite the suppression, some monks remained, and in the reign of Elizabeth, c. 1561, twelve monks were murdered outside the Abbey.

In 1728 a thatched Masshouse was erected within the Abbey walls. In 1744 the great octagonal tower collapsed, bringing down the stone roof of the chancel and part of the nave arcade. In 1754 the west end of the Abbey was re-roofed by members of the established Church. Lord Dover granted a lease for ever to the Parish Priest and people of Graig of the chapel and Abbey ruins, in 1809. Some building work followed which was, unfortunately, not in line with the walls of the west end of the nave.

In 1973 it was decided to restore the Abbey church. The architect was Mr. Percy Le Clerc, with Fr. Patrick Dunny C.C. as co-ordinator. The work was to include removal of the galleries, re-ordering of the interior, removal of the cross-wall that cut off the arcades which had remained at the western end and the construction of an entirely new roof at the original pitch. Oak and elm were donated from woods at Knocktopher, Abbeyleix, Gowran and Waterford. The original system of roofing with unseasoned timber using wooden pegs was followed. The central oak pendant over the sanctuary weighs over a ton, and was cut from a tree in Knocktopher forest. Liscannor slate was used and windows were restored. On 1st June 1980 the Abbey was reopened for use. The sanctuary cross (1990) is by Brother Benedict Tutty O.S.B.

The Porchway and west end of the North Aisle were rebuilt in 1983. The arches of the south transept were blocked up until 1987. The "Our Lady of Duiske" icon is by Sr. Paula, Glencairn Abbey (1988), and the Emmaus Scene by Sr. Rosaleen McCabe, St. Clare Sisters (1991). The windows in the south wall and the lancet glass in the chancel are the work of Patrick Pollen. The bronze lid of the baptismal font is by Seán Adamson (1990), and the Baptism of Jesus plaque by Betty Ryan (1988).

Our Lady of Lourdes, Skeoughvosteen

DATE OF CHURCH: C. 1825
STYLE: CRUCIFORM

SKEOUGHVOSTEEN (*SCEACH AN MHAISTIN*. *SCEACH*, THORNBUSH, BRIAR; *MAISTIN*, MASTIFF, FIERCE DOG; A BULLY; SCREAMING CHILD).

THE CHURCH has shortened transepts and very unusual sloping, stepped side-aisles like galleries at ground level. It has lovely yellow granite in all four portals. The beautiful interior was greatly enhanced by the re-ordering of the 1990's.

The erection of the new church in the 1820's probably coincided with the formation of the new parish of Goresbridge and Paulstown in 1822. The Goresbridge church replaced an older one at Powerstown, now on the edge of the two parishes.

Bishop Thomas Keogh (1936-1967) was a native of Skeoughvosteen.

Our Lady of Lourdes, Skeoughvosteen

John Duffy

Parish of Myshall

CLERGY IN THE PARISH IN THE YEAR 2000
V. REV. PHILIP O'SHEA P.P.
REV. BRENDAN HOWARD C.C.

CATHOLIC POPULATION: 1,300

Church of Exaltation of the Holy Cross, Myshall

DATE OF CHURCH: c. 1776
STYLE: CRUCIFORM

MYSHALL (*MUIGH ÍSEAL,* THE LOW PLAIN).

THE VILLAGE OF MYSHALL lies at the foot of Mount Leinster. The ancient church of St. Finian was founded at Myshall and the ruins of it still remain. St. Finian was from the area and studied under St. Fortchern in Killoughternane. He later founded monasteries at Aghowle and Clonard.

The site granted for the church was a swamp, but was still regarded as a generous concession by the landlord. The belfry was built in 1900. The church itself is a small structure built of rough stone and lime mortar.

Liturgical changes took place in 1974 with the installation of a new altar, tabernacle place, ambo, and a new floor. The church was rededicated in 1976 when its Bicentenary was celebrated. In 2000 a Jubilee Cross was erected in the grounds of Holy Cross Church in a new Garden of Remembrance.

Dr. Joseph Byrne, who bequeathed a fortune to his native parish

Dr. Joseph Byrne, native of Myshall parish, was an eminent New York surgeon. Prior to his death in 1945, he made a bequest to his native parish for the purpose of assisting the educational needs of its children. The resulting fund (worth £772,710 in 1993) is administered by the Byrne Trust.

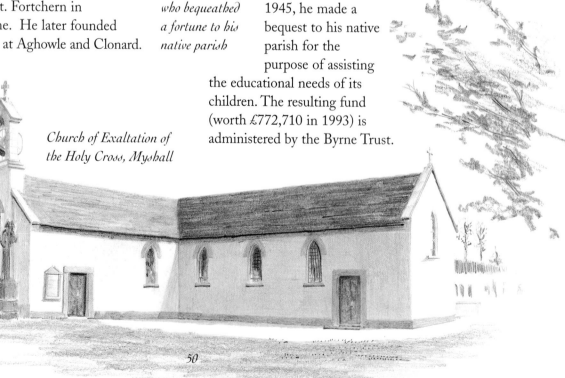

Church of Exaltation of the Holy Cross, Myshall

St Laserian's Church, Drumphea

St Laserian's Church, Drumphea

> DATE OF CHURCH: 1810
> STYLE: CRUCIFORM
> BUILDING PASTOR: FR. JOHN CLEARY P.P.

DRUMPHEA
(THE RIDGE OF THE DEER; *DROIM*, RIDGE; *FIA*, DEER).

THE KAVANAGHS OF BORRIS held the castle of Rathnageera as an out-fort from the 13th century to 1631. Destroyed by Cromwell's forces in 1650, the castle and surrounding lands were granted to Sir Richard Kennedy.

The church of St. Laserian is situated in the Blackstairs Mountains, and was built on the foundations of an earlier church. A foundation stone states: "To the honour and glory of God this chapel was built by the Rev. J.C. P.P. and the liberal subscriptions of the Parishioners, A.D. 1810". Classes were conducted in the Chapel by a Mr John Kelly in the early 19th century. The belfry was built in 1900 by Fr. Richard O'Brien, and the grotto in 1954. A new roof was added in the 1940s. The church was renovated according to the design of Ray Carroll.

In 1989 wood rot was discovered. Major renovations took place under architect Roger Patterson and builders Lalor Brothers. The work of re-roofing, lighting, painting, carpentry etc., was carried out, under Fr. John Hayden, P.P. The re-dedication was performed on Sunday 24th February 1991 by Bishop Laurence Ryan.

The church has a chalice given by Mgr. William Farrell, Canada, on the occasion of his Silver Jubilee in 1990. A monument to Capt. James Nolan, 1798 Rebel, was erected in Drumphea Cemetery, where he is interred.

Parish of Muine Bheag (Bagenalstown)

CLERGY IN THE PARISH IN THE YEAR 2000
V. REV. PIERCE MURPHY. P.P., V.F.
V. REV. EDWARD DOWLING P.E., C.C.
REV. THOMAS BAMBRICK S.M., C.C.
REV. KEVIN WALSH C.C.

CATHOLIC POPULATION: 5,500

St. Andrew's Church, Muine Bheag

DATE OF THE CHURCH: 1820
BUILDING PASTOR: FR. MICHAEL PRENDERGAST
ARCHITECT: THOMAS COBDEN (PRESUMED)
SANCTUARY (1893): WILLIAM HAGUE

MUINE BHEAG (*MUINE*, A SHRUBBERY, SMALL WOODED AREA).

Dunleckney House, home of the Bagenals

BAGENALSTOWN was named after the town's founder, Walter Bagenal of Dunleckney. Walter Bagenal set about designing and building a town of considerable dimensions which he intended to name New Versailles, but a change in the route of the coach-road to crossing the River Barrow at Leighlinbridge put paid to his fine plans.

Ruins of St. Fortchern's Church, Killoughternane

The site for the church was provided c. 1814 by the Newton family, successors to the Bagenals. The facade was delicately carved in local stone, which came from Hogan's quarry, Boherduff, and was dressed in New St., Muine Bheag. Building took three years from 1817.

The church was renovated in 1893, when the sanctuary was added. The high altar was erected under the direction of Fr Bernard O'Neill. About 1917 the porches in the side aisles were added, the builder being a brother of Bishop Patrick Foley.

The Mortuary was added in Mgr. James Conway's time as P.P. (1948-1976), and in 1978 the Sanctuary was re-ordered, under Fr. Edward Dowling.

The Batik hangings are by Bernadette Madden, and the large hanging cross in enamels and beaten bronze is by Patrick McElroy. The stained glass behind the altar is worthy of particular attention.

St. Andrew's, Bagenalstown

St. Patrick's Church, Newtown

DATE OF THE CHURCH: 1832
ARCHITECT: THOMAS COBDEN (POSSIBLY)
BUILDING PASTOR: FR. ML. PRENDERGAST, P.P.

NEWTOWN (*AN BAILE NUA*)

BEGUN IN 1832 AND FINISHED IN 1884, Newtown church is described in Williams' 'Architecture in Ireland 1837-1921' as "a high-spirited church, a reduced version of Cobden's Carlow Cathedral, lovingly preserved even to its fretwork confessionals. Cruciform externally, articulated by diagonal pinnacles, the sophisticated planning gives direct access to three galleries: the main gallery, extending more than half-way down the nave is supported by two rows of clustered columns - a church within a church".

The granite stone was quarried in nearby Boherduff. Italian artisans, who worked on local 'Big Houses' are thought to have done the church ceiling. The roof was a gift of the Broughan family of Ballybromhill. The altar and steps were a gift of the Kinsella, Hughes, and Rafter families.
The mosaics at the back of the altar and outside were added in the 1950's. The church possesses stained glass windows by Joshua Clarke. In 2000 there are plans for refurbishment and conservation work.

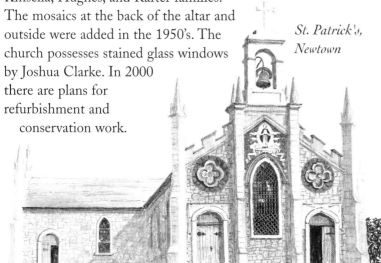

St. Patrick's, Newtown

St. Laserian's, Ballinkillen

St. Laserian's Church, Ballinkillen

DATE OF THE CHURCH: 1793
BUILDING PASTOR: FR. MICHAEL BROPHY
STYLE: CRUCIFORM
SEATING: 300

BALLINKILLEN (*BAILE AN CHUILINN*, TOWN OF THE HOLLY).

THIS CHURCH is one of the oldest in the Diocese and bears the inscription "Presented by the parishioners of Ballinkillen to Rev. Michael Brophy, 1776". An ancient graveyard and ruins at Lorum mark the site of the previous Catholic church.

In 1915 work began on a new roof. The wooden altar was replaced by one of white marble, a gift of the Maher family of Ballyellen. This altar was replaced in 1978, in accordance with the reforms of Vatican II; a fine granite altar is now used. The architrave of the high altar was preserved. The church grounds were improved in 1989 by voluntary labour. The Calvary in the churchyard was erected to the memory of Fr. Thomas Seale, C.C. who died in 1935. Mrs. Maeve Hughes donated the site for the Lourdes Grotto, which was blessed on 1 October 1989. Buried at Ballinkillen is Teresa Malone, heroine of the battle of Kilcumney, in 1798.

Parish of Paulstown

CLERGY IN THE PARISH IN THE YEAR 2000
V. REV. JIM O'CONNELL P.P.
V. REV. SEAN Ó LAOGHAIRE P.E., C.C.

CATHOLIC POPULATION: 1,700

Church of the Assumption, Paulstown

DATE OF CHURCH: 1796
BUILDING PASTOR: FR. WILLIAM CULLEN, LEIGHLIN
STYLE: CRUCIFORM VERNACULAR

PAULSTOWN (*BAILE PHÓIL*; A TOWNSLAND IN AN AREA OF
THE SHANKILL DEMESNE; AT ONE TIME PAULSTOWN HAD
A CASTLE SAID TO BE BUILT BY THE KELLYS).
IN SHANKILL, (*SEAN CHILL, OLD CHURCH*), THE RUINS OF THE
OLD PAROCHIAL CHURCH STAND IN THE DEMESNE,
CLOSE TO THE OLD RESIDENCE OF THE AYLWARDS.

TWO SAINTS, Enda and Lochan, are associated with Kilmacahill. Lochan was son of Cathal, hence *Cill mac Cathal*. The old monastery site is in the townland of Kellymount.

Dr. Comerford records a foundation stone with the following inscription: "The half-acre on which this chapel is built, is given gratis for ever, by Charles Stanly Monk, Esq., for the use of the Roman Catholic inhabitants of the united parishes of Kilmacahill, Shankill, and Wells, with a free donation of forty guineas for its building, the remainder by the voluntary contributions of the inhabitants of the above mentioned parishes. Rev. William Cullen, R.C. Pastor, 1796".

This foundation stone was rediscovered in 1997 by Mr. Michael Regan, Contractor, of Graiguecullen, while employed to re-slate the church roof. It is now mounted in the porch. Re-roofing at this time cost £35,800.

Paulstown church is the oldest surviving example in Co. Kilkenny of an 18th century chapel. It was originally dedicated to St. Paul. Fr. Richard O'Brien changed the dedication soon after 1901. The limestone and granite porches were erected in 1906 in memory of Fr. Patrick Mulhall P.P. (1870-1901).

The bell was purchased in 1876 for £30, and an altar installed in 1881 cost £70. Three confessionals were bought in 1886 for £16.10s. In 1890, a new organ cost £62.

The present altar, ambo, chair and tabernacle stand in Kellymount limestone, the work of Domhnal McDonald. These were dedicated in 1981.

Church of the Assumption, Paulstown

Very Rev. Richard O'Brien, from Killeenmore, Killeigh, Co. Offaly, was P.P. 1901-1934. He was responsible for a lot of work including the erection of the porches and belfry. He collected funds to contest the conscription of Irishmen into the British Army during the First World War. When this danger had passed, the money was used to build a new play shed in the school grounds. He is buried at the Lourdes Grotto at the rear of the church.

Very Rev. Richard O'Brien, Parish Priest (1901-1934)

In 1798, the Wexford Rebels, led by Fr. John Murphy captured Goresbridge on their way to Castlecomer. Receiving little support, they returned, intent on re-entering Co. Wexford. The group were attacked at nearby Kilcumney Hill on 26th June by Sir Charles Asgill of Kilkenny. Many local non-combatants were killed.

The church is a simple building, cruciform in shape. Prior to this, a humble chapel stood a little to the right of the present entrance.

As in Paulstown the porches were erected in 1906 as a memorial to Fr. Mulhall. The present marble altar and ambo were moved from the convent chapel on its closure in 1970. This district, part of Graignamanagh parish until 1822, formed part of the old parish of Grange Silvae, which had its church at Upper Grange.

Holy Trinity Church, Goresbridge

DATE OF CHURCH: C. 1813
BUILDING PASTOR: FR. LEWIS MOORE, GRAIGNAMANAGH
STYLE: CRUCIFORM VERNACULAR

To the south of Barrowmount is Killeen, where a small graveyard has a Gore family vault. Mass was offered in Penal times at the Mass Bush in Barrowmount.

A convent was established by the Brigidine Sisters in Goresbridge in 1858; they also established a branch-house at Paulstown.

GORESBRIDGE, named after the Gore family, who arrived at the end of the 17th century, and the bridge over the River Barrow, which links Counties Kilkenny and Carlow. An alternate name was Newbridge. The Gores were originally from Lecum in Hertfordshire.

Holy Trinity Church, Goresbridge

Parish of Leighlin

PARISH PRIEST IN THE YEAR 2000
V. REV. THOMAS LALOR P.P.

CATHOLIC POPULATION: 2,500

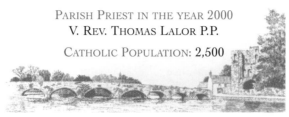

The focal point of Leighlin is its bridge and castle

St. Laserian's, Leighlinbridge

DATE OF CHURCH: c. 1770
STYLE: CRUCIFORM
RENOVATION ARCHITECT: COLM HASSETT
RENOVATION COST: £230,000

LEIGHLINBRIDGE is about 4 Km from Old Leighlin and is situated on the River Barrow. It was originally called New Leighlin prior to the building of the first stone bridge over the river by Maurice Jakis, a Canon of the Cathedral of Kildare, in 1320. Leighlinbridge has been regarded as one of the most important river crossings in Ireland for more than a thousand years. For a long period of time the River Barrow was the limit of the Pale. The crossing was controlled by the McMurrough Kavanaghs who extracted payment from the Crown for safe passage.

The Carmelites had a monastery near the Black Castle, on the east bank of the River Barrow, founded by one of the Carews. This lasted until c. 1828.

Before the construction of the present church of St. Laserian, a penal-day chapel existed in Conicare which was probably thatched with mud walls. The spot is known as "the church field".

The present church was constructed of rubble stone with granite door, window jambs and mullions.

Fr. Patrick Kehoe P.P. (1827-1858) had the church raised and re-roofed. Fr. James Connolly P.P. (1890-1897) added the altar area, sacristy and granite decorations. Generous donations were made by two illustrious native sons: Cardinal Moran, Archbishop of Sydney presented a marble altar, while Bishop Patrick Foley, Bishop of Kildare and Leighlin (1896-1926) sponsored the communion rails. Australia's first Cardinal, Patrick Francis Moran (1830-1911), born at Bridge St., Leighlinbridge, was appointed Bishop of Ossory in 1872, and Archbishop of Sydney in 1884.

St. Laserian's, Leighlinbridge

Cardinal Moran, native of Leighlinbridge

John Duffy

The bell tower, which differs in architectural style from the church, is thought to be much older than St. Laserian's, but information on it is scanty.

On Sunday 9th June 1985, Bishop Patrick Lennon blessed the re-ordered St. Laserian's.

St. Fintan's Church, Ballinabranna

DATE OF CHURCH: C. 1820
BUILDING PASTOR: FR. WILLIAM CULLEN P.P.
RENOVATION ARCHITECT: COLM HASSETT
COST OF RENOVATION: £130,000

BALLINABRANNA
(TOWN OF THE BREATHNACHS OR WALSHES).

THE SITE FOR ST. FINTAN'S was granted by the Alexander family of Milford. An earlier church, St. Brigid's in Tomard stood near St. Brigid's well.
In August 1983, Bishop Patrick Lennon blessed the re-ordered church. The sculptured granite altar was complemented by the unusual Baptismal font, also of granite. The design on the wooden cross was repeated in the panelled sides of the presider's chair. The Tabernacle is on the marble altar presented to the church by Cardinal Moran. New seating was also installed, and the porch and choir gallery were removed. The water font in the porch bears the following inscription: "The gift of William Cullen sculptor to the Rev. Anthony Goss 1824".

John Conwill, a teacher in the school in the church grounds, taught John Tyndall between 1836 and 1838. Tyndall, native of Main St. Leighlinbridge, was one of the most outstanding achievers of his age and gained a world-wide reputation as a scientist, educationalist, inventor, and mountain climber.

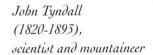

John Tyndall (1820-1893), scientist and mountaineer

St. Fintan's Church, Ballinabranna

LEIGHLIN CATHEDRAL

Church of Ireland

THE HISTORY OF LEIGHLIN CATHEDRAL stretches back to the early 7th century when St. Gobban founded a monastery here, in what is now the village of Old Leighlin.

Aside from its obvious architectural interest, the Cathedral is famed for its connection with St. Laserian who played a major part in the decision within the Celtic Church to adopt the Roman method of calculating the date for Easter at the synod of Leighlin in 630 A.D.

Laserian, who succeeded Gobban as abbot, had previously spent fourteen years in Rome where Gregory the Great had ordained him. On a further visit to Rome in 633, Pope Honorius I consecrated him as first Bishop of Leighlin. The monastery, which was reported to have 1,500 monks, was made the principal seat of the Episcopal See. Laserian died on 18th April 639.

The original Cathedral was possibly constructed of wood. The Danes plundered the Cathedral twice, in 859 and 916. It was also attacked in 982 by the Chief of Ossory. Bishop Donatus rebuilt it at the end of the 12th century, a construction which included the long chancel and nave of the present building to which two transepts north and south were soon added. The northern one is now roofless while no trace remains of the southern one.

The late Gothic alterations were done by Bishop Matthew Sanders (1529-1549) whose tomb is near the sanctuary. The alterations include the insertion of the tower, the addition of a chapel north of the chancel – which is now the chapter room – and partial rebuilding of the north and south chancel walls. A later addition was the splendid wooden ceiling of the chancel inserted in 1899.

A unique feature of the Cathedral is its very fine sedilia – a row of seats in the wall of the choir for the use of officiating clergy – dating from the 13th century. Usually there are three seats, but Leighlin boasts the only four bay structure extant in Ireland. The reason for this departure from custom is now unknown.

The oldest item in the Cathedral is probably the 11th century font in the chancel. Its simple severe design is in marked contrast to a second font dating from 1225 A.D. standing by the main door. This latter font, which was originally in St. Mary's Church in Gowran, is richly decorated with stone carving known as Ossory fluting.

Leighlin Cathedral

We are very grateful to Rev. Ken Sherwood, Old Leighlin, for providing this introduction to Leighlin Cathedral – Editor.

PORTLAOISE DEANERY

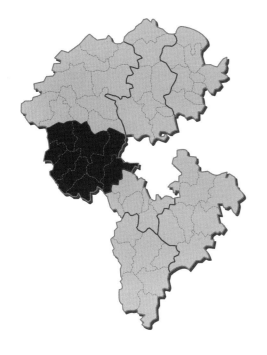

PARISHES

PORTLAOISE	60, 61
STRADBALLY	62, 63
BALLYADAMS	64, 65
BALLINAKILL	66, 67
ABBEYLEIX	68, 69
RAHEEN	70, 71
MOUNTRATH	72, 73
BALLYFIN	74

CLERGY IN THE PARISH IN THE YEAR 2000
V. REV. JOHN BYRNE P.P.
REV. LIAM MERRIGAN C.C.
REV. PAUL FITZPATRICK C.C.
REV. PATRICK BANVILLE C.C.
REV. GREGORY CORCORAN C.C.

CATHOLIC POPULATION: 9,600

S.S. Peter & Paul Church, Portlaoise

DATE OF CHURCH: 1965
STYLE: GOTHIC
ARCHITECT: JONES & KELLY
BUILDING PASTOR: FR. THOMAS BROWNE P.P.
SEATING: 1,800

S.S. Peter & Paul Church, Portlaoise

MARYBOROUGH / PORTLAOISE
(*PORT LAOIGHISE,* FORT - LEIX).

THE ANCIENT NAME for this town was Campa, and is referred to in the Annals of the Four Masters, in 1548: "O'Conor and O'More went to England with the Lieutenant (Francis Bryan), at the King's mercy. The King, however, gave their patrimonial inheritance, namely, Leix & Offaly, to the Lieutenant and his kinsmen, who built two large courts in these territories, namely Campa in Leix, and Philipstown (now Daingean) in Offaly". The O'Conors and O'Mores were then banished. An Act of Parliament was passed in 1556 (Reign of Philip & Mary) "that the new Fort in Laoise be, from henceforth for ever, called Mary Burgh".
A Gothic-style church was built in Portlaoise in the early 19th century by Fr. Nicholas O'Connor. The site for the present church was acquired c. 1908 by Mgr. Michael Murphy P.P. V.G.

when he bought Dr. Jacob's house, and its garden on the far side of the street.

The modern parish church is a very large structure in red brick. The builders were Messrs. Jennings Ltd. of Dun Laoghaire. The opening ceremony was performed by Monsignor James Conway in September 1965.

The bell, baptismal font, tabernacle, holy water font and other items, were transferred from the old church. The windows are very beautiful, depicting the rising sun, in coloured glass.

Fr. Thomas Browne P.P., who built the church, had been President of St. Patrick's College, Carlow and was P.P. in Portlaoise 1941-1976. He died in 1982 aged 97. Corrective work was carried out on the tower in 1990.

Church of the Assumption,
The Heath

Church of the Assumption, The Heath

DATE OF CHURCH: 1836
STYLE: RECTANGULAR
BUILDING PASTOR: FR. NICHOLAS O'CONNOR P.P.

THE HEATH (*AN FRAOCH MÓR*, THE BIG HEATH.
MOY RETA, OR THE PLAIN OF RIATA, WAS THE NAME OF
AN EXTENSIVE PLAIN IN THE COUNTY OF LEIX.)

AN EARLIER CHURCH stood on the Ballydavis side of The Heath. The present large building is rectangular and constructed from cut stone. The front has three entrance doors over which are three gothic windows. Above the central window is a stone in memory of the church's builder, Fr. Nicholas O'Connor.

The Tabernacle and a large silver Crucifix came from the old S.S. Peter & Paul Church at Portlaoise. An attractive feature of the Church is a three-dimensional ceiling painting.

The side windows were installed in the 1940's. The Baptismal Font is in memory of Fr. Joseph Farrell, a noted preacher, who served as curate in Maryborough (1871-1878).
In 1999, under the direction of Msgr. T. Coonan P.P., the church was painted and re-carpeted.

Holy Cross, Ratheniska

DATE OF CHURCH: 1800
STYLE: CRUCIFORM
BUILDING PASTOR: FR. JAMES O'NEILL P.P.

RATHENISKA (*RATH AN UISCE*), FORT/RATH OF THE WATER).
THE RATH REFERRED TO ONCE OCCUPIED PORTION OF A
FARMER'S FIELD NEAR THE CHURCH.

ST. AONGHUS, born c. 750, studied at the monastery of Clonenagh. He came to live the life of a hermit in Dysart, overlooking Ratheniska. He erected a cell there known as Diseart-Aonghusa. At Tallaght he wrote his famous work: the 'Féilire Aonghusa'.

The site for the church was given by Lord Castletown. The church is a small building typical of the period. It has been refurbished several times. A modern sanctuary was provided in the 1980's.

The church was re-decorated for the celebration of its Bicentenary in June 2000.

Holy Cross, Ratheniska

Parish of Stradbally

CLERGY IN THE PARISH IN THE YEAR 2000
V. REV. SEAN KELLY P.P.
REV. PATRICK BREEN C.C.

CATHOLIC POPULATION: 2,800

Sacred Heart, Stradbally

DATE OF CHURCH: 1896
STYLE: CRUCIFORM
ARCHITECT: WILLIAM HAGUE
BUILDING PASTOR: FR. MICHAEL BRENNAN P.P.

STRADBALLY (*BAILE,* TOWN; *SRÁID,* A STREET; A SINGLE STREET VILLAGE).

ST. COLEMAN, who had been educated at Iona under St. Columba, founded a monastery at Oughaval. The site was later occupied by the parochial church.

A Franciscan monastery was established in the 13th century at Stradbally. In a Return of 1731, it is stated: "Stradbally, Fossey, Timmogue: One Mass House, built within ten years. One Schoolmaster, James Walsh; Priests, Pat Kelly and John Burn, ye sd John Burn came lately from France, frequently officiates in sd Mass House and in sev'll private houses".

In 1796 Admiral Cosby granted a lease of a site in Cushen's yard for a church.

Fr. George Hume P.P. 1850-1862 welcomed Presentation Sisters to Stradbally in 1852. The Sisters educated the poor and ran a large orphanage. They donated the site for the new Church. The Church of the Sacred Heart is a fine imposing structure. (President Mary McAleese unveiled a plaque in Butlersbridge, Co. Cavan in memory of the Architect Hague in 1999. When he died in 1889, aged 63, he had designed over 200 public buildings).

In 1996, the people of Stradbally erected a centenary stone in the grounds of the Church.

Sacred Heart, Stradbally

John Duffy

Church of the Assumption,
Vicarstown

Church of the Assumption, Vicarstown

DATE OF CHURCH: 1841
BUILDING PASTOR: FR. CORNELIUS DOWLING P.P.

VICARSTOWN (*BAILE AN BHIOCÁIRE*, TOWN OF THE VICAR).

THE BRANCH OF THE GRAND CANAL through Vicarstown opened in 1791, and offered transport of goods and comfortable passage for travellers.

The church of the Assumption is a large, slated, cruciform structure of stone, surmounted by a large stone cross. The front portion, facing the gateway to the church, is un-plastered and consists of regular blocks of cut stone in the wall and corner pillars. The windows are of Gothic design with the largest positioned above the entrance doorway.

St. Michael's, Timahoe

DATE OF CHURCH: 1832
STYLE: GOTHIC
BUILDING PASTOR: FR. CORNELIUS DOWLING P.P.

TIMAHOE (*TEACH MOCHUA*, HOUSE OF ST. MOCHUA, FOUNDER AND PATRON, WHO FLOURISHED IN THE 7TH CENTURY).

TIMAHOE IS SITUATED IN FOSSEY, the ancient parochial district, the ruins of its church being to the south-east of the village. A religious community existed in Timahoe as late as 1650.

The round tower of Timahoe is built of limestone and the openings are of sandstone. The tower is 96ft in height and 57ft in circumference at the base, and the wall is 4ft. thick. There are five stories above the floor level.

Fr. Dowling, who presided over the building of the Church, is buried within its walls. The church's stained glass windows are worthy of particular attention.

On a farm at Garryglass, Timahoe, owned by a Mr. Mooney, is a holy well overhung by a Mass-bush, called St. Cornelius's Well. A member of the Mooney family discovered a chalice there along with what is thought to be the remnants of a timber altar.

St. Michael's,
Timahoe

Round Tower,
Timahoe

Parish of Ballyadams

PARISH PRIEST IN THE YEAR 2000
V. REV. JAMES DOYLE P.P.

CATHOLIC POPULATION: 1,500

St Joseph's Church, Ballyadams

DATE OF CHURCH: C. 1840
STYLE: CRUCIFORM
BUILDING PASTOR: FR. MAURICE HARTE P.P.
RENOVATION ARCHITECT: PATRICIA ENNIS, KILDARE

BALLYADAMS (*BAILE ADAM;* TOWN OF ADAM.
ADAM UNKNOWN). AN ALTERNATIVE NAME WAS *KILMAKEADY,*
THE CHURCH OF THE FLAT-TOPPED HILL.

THE CASTLE OF BALLYADAMS, an O'More stronghold, was taken by the Geraldines in the rebellion of Silken Thomas.

The church of St. Joseph replaced an earlier thatched chapel. It is a small structure built of local stone, and has a single gallery. The exposed stone in the interior is particularly attractive. The 'Gospel' side aisle was added c. 1860. Renovations were carried out in 1998.
The builder was Mr. Sydney Strong, of Portlaoise. During renovations in Ballyadams, all church services were held in the nearby Church of Ireland at Ballintubbert.

St. Mary's Church, Wolfhill

DATE OF CHURCH: C. 1860
STYLE: BARN-TYPE
BUILDING PASTOR: FR. EDWARD FENLON P.P.

WOLFHILL (*CNOCÁN NA MACTIRE,*
LITTLE HILL OF THE WOLVES).

WOLFHILL CHURCH is a large structure built with local stone. It is said to have been built over a period of seven years, mostly summer work. Fr. Fenlon P.P. donated most of the cost of the original building. The Grace family of Gracefield House donated the roof.

St Joseph's Church, Ballyadams

John Delby

St. Mary's Church, Wolfhill

In 1979-1980, renovations took place under architect Mr. Michael Crowe. The builder was Mr. Michael Regan. The cost of the work was £110,000. The interior stone walls were pointed in 1964 by Andy Morrin and cost £3,034.

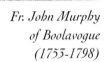

Fr. John Murphy of Boolavogue (1753-1798)

The stained glass window over the altar was destroyed in the Big Wind of 1903. The present window was installed in that year and was the gift of Fr. James Parkinson, P.P. (1900-1920).

Nearby is a plaque erected by the Wolfhill '98 committee stating that the area of Slatt Lower was where Fr. John Murphy and Wexford Rebels camped in June 1798. This was the furthest that this group had travelled, and failing to find support in the midlands they headed back towards Wexford.

Holy Rosary Church, Luggacurren

> DATE OF CHURCH: C. 1825
> BUILDING PASTOR: FR. MAURICE HARTE P.P.

LUGGACURREN (*LOG AN CHURRAIGH*; *LOG*, A HOLLOW; *CARAGH*, AN AREA WITH AN O'KELLY CASTLE).

THE O'KELLY'S ancient territory, shown on an old map of Leix and Offaly, extended from Ballymaddock southwards to the hills of Slievemargy, comprising Ballymaddock, the Park, the churches of Grange and Oghteoge, the church of Clopoke, and the Castle of Coragh. The ancient church still exists in ruins. Many priests were buried there during the 18th century.

The church of the Holy Rosary is said to have been built c. 1825. Renovations were conducted in 1994 under the direction of Ms Patricia Ennis, architect, Kildare, and builder Mr. Michael Knowles, of Wolfhill.

Holy Rosary Church, Luggacurren

Parish of Ballinakill

CLERGY IN THE PARISH IN THE YEAR 2000
V. REV. S. CONLON P.P.
SIX PRIESTS FROM SALESIAN HOUSE, BALLINAKILL.

CATHOLIC POPULATION: 1,400

St. Brigid's Church, Ballinakill

DATE OF CHURCH: 1806
BUILDING PASTOR: DR. WILLIAM CAHILL P.P.

BALLINAKILL IS SITUATED IN THE ANCIENT PAROCHIAL DISTRICT OF DYSERT GALLEN.
(*BAILE NA COILLE*, THE TOWN OF THE WOOD, NAMED AFTER THE EXTENSIVE WOODS WHICH FORMERLY EXISTED IN THE AREA).

Salesian Chapel now forms part of the new Heywood Community School (1990). The School, with about 650 pupils, occupies the site of the original Heywood Mansion. The Province of the Irish Salesian Fathers acquired Heywood in 1941 and opened a Juniorate there. Unfortunately the House was destroyed by fire in 1950. The Luytens Gardens have been restored and form part of the Laois Heritage Trail.

I N HEYWOOD DEMESNE exists the site of a humble thatched church which pre-dates the present parish church. The adjoining lake was referred to as the Mass Lough, a reference to the celebration of Mass in Penal times.

The site for St. Brigid's was leased from Miss E. Trench, of Heywood House, Ballinakill. The church was built with stone and mortar, and has Gothic-style windows. The main building was constructed in 1806. The porch and belfry were added in 1854, and the vestries in 1900.

The present organ was purchased in 1987 from the Irish Christian Brothers Novitiate at Booterstown, Dublin. The three large stained glass windows in the rear wall were donated by a local businessman, Mr. P.J. Byrne, in 1894. Major interior work took place in 1970.

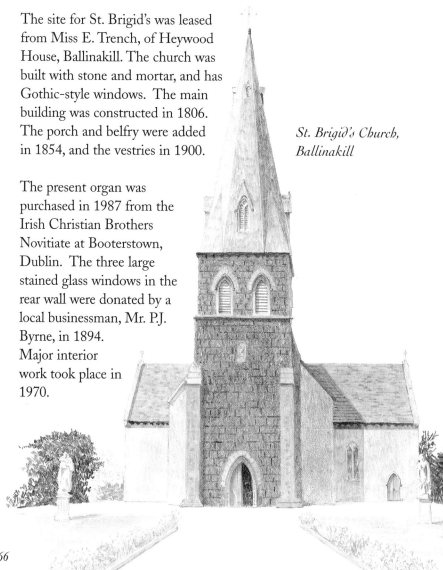

St. Brigid's Church, Ballinakill

St. Laserian's Church,
Knock

St. Laserian's Church, Knock

DATE OF CHURCH: 1849
BUILDING PASTOR: FR. JAMES DELANEY P.P.
STYLE: CRUCIFORM

KNOCK (*CNOC*, HILL).

O N A HILL ABOVE DYSERT-GALLEN, called *Knockardagur*, there once stood a castle, traces of which have faded with time. Reference exists, however, to one Barnaby Dempsye, of Knockardagur, in the Queen's County, who lived here. His name appears in the list of "Proclaimed traitors and rebels, 1641-2". He was tried and executed in Kilkenny in 1652.

The church is built on land made available by Rev. Charles Doyne. The building, constructed from stone and mortar is a large cruciform structure described by Comerford as "one of the handsomest country chapels in the county". Work on the church began in 1841 and was completed in 1849.

The Lourdes Grotto in the church grounds was donated by the O'Connor family, Spink. The church was refurbished in 1972.

Stone carved heads on doorway of
St. Laserian's

Parish of Abbeyleix

CLERGY IN THE PARISH IN THE YEAR 2000
V. REV. PATRICK KEHOE P.P.
REV. JAMES KELLY C.C.

CATHOLIC POPULATION: 3,000

Holy Rosary Church, Abbeyleix

DATE OF CHURCH: 1895
STYLE: CRUCIFORM, ROMANESQUE
ARCHITECT: WILLIAM HAGUE
BUILDERS: STEPHEN LALOR, KILKENNY
BUILDING PASTOR: FR. JAMES LALOR, P.P.

ABBEYLEIX (*MAINISTIR LAOIGHISE*, THE ABBEY OF LEIX, SO CALLED FROM A MONASTERY FOUNDED THERE IN 1183 BY CONOR O'MORE).

THIS ABBEY was Cistercian and was founded from Baltinglass. A religious community is said to have been here since the year 600.

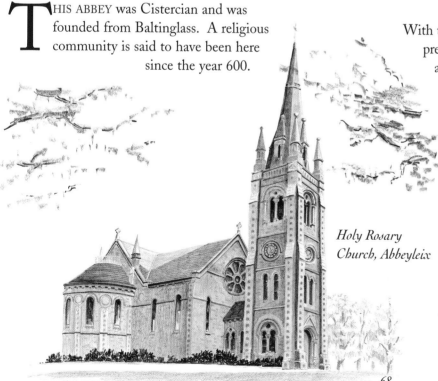

Holy Rosary Church, Abbeyleix

The old town of Abbeyleix grew around the 12th century Abbey, on what was later to become the De Vesci demesne. In the early 1800's Lord De Vesci levelled old Abbeyleix and laid out the present town on a superior site. The O'More chieftains were buried in the locality of the abbey.

In 1588, three Franciscan priests, John O'Mulloy, Cornelius Dogherty, and Calfrid Ferrall, were captured by a party of cavalry in a remote part of Queen's County. They were outlawed priests, ministering to their flock in secret. They were brought to the garrison at Abbeyleix where they were tortured and hanged.

Bishop James Doyle (J.K.L.) formed the new parish of Abbeyleix in 1824. Previously the area formed part of Ballinakill parish.

With the construction of the new town a chapel was built on the present site of the Most Holy Rosary Church. This was also a De Vesci site.

Holy Rosary church has architectural round arches throughout and is in the shape of a Latin Cross. The external walls are faced with hammered ashlar and have limestone chiselled dressings. The church foundation stone reads "Ecclesia Sacratissimi Rosarii. Abbeyleix 1893".

The bell, which weighs 29 cwts., was erected in 1906. In 1993 the sanctuary area was re-ordered and thorough renovations were carried out. The church has three altars - a high altar and two side altars, which are now shrines. All are made of marble, with coloured shafts.

St. Patrick's Church, Ballyroan

John Duffy

St. Patrick's Church, Ballyroan

DATE OF CHURCH: 1840
STYLE: BARN-TYPE, GOTHIC
BUILDING PASTOR: FR. THOMAS NOLAN P.P.

BALLYROAN (*BAILE ÁTHA NA RÓINE*. AN OLD STORY SAYS THAT WHEN THE NORMANS SAW THE GLOREEN RIVER THEY CALLED IT LE RHONE. OTHER NAME THEORIES EXIST, BUT A RIVER CONNECTION IS MOST PLAUSIBLE, ESPECIALLY AS THE IRISH WORD *ATH* MEANS 'FORD').

ST. FAOLAN founded a monastery here c. 468, at Kilphelan - about a mile and a half north of Ballyroan.

A manuscript in Trinity College, Dublin, states that a castle once existed in Ballyroan. It translates, "Conall, the son of David O'More, King of Leix, re-erected the castle of Dunamase after having taken it from the English, and built the castle of Baile-atha-in-Roine and replanted with his own people every part of his territory".

Rory Óg O' More

Near Ballyroan the Battle of Bearna na gCleti or the "Pass of Plumes" was fought in 1599, when Owny MacRory O'More defeated the Earl of Essex. In 1999 a monumental garden was arranged at Cashel Cross to mark the event's fourth centenary.

St. Patrick's Church, built of stone, is a sizeable, well-proportioned structure, rectangular in shape, with a fine steeple. The external walls have been cement plastered. In the grounds of the church a large rock, placed there in 1990, bears the inscription: "St. Patrick's Church, Ballyroan, 1840".

Parish of Raheen

PARISH PRIEST IN THE YEAR 2000
V. REV. THOMAS DILLON P.P., V.F.

CATHOLIC POPULATION: 1,200

St. Fintan's Church, Raheen

DATE OF CHURCH: 1860
STYLE: RECTANGULAR

RAHEEN (THE LITTLE FORT).

UNTIL THE YEAR 1820, the parish of Raheen was part of the extensive district of Clonenagh. Old church ruins exist at Cromogue where, it is said, St. Fintan resided before founding his monastery at Clonenagh c. 548. St. Fintan is thought to be from Clonkeen, Co. Laois. His monastery was amongst the prime centres of learning and was called the Gallic school, from the large number of foreign attendants, especially from Gaul. Nearby is St. Fintan's well - pebbles from the well are said to protect against shipwreck or accidental death.

The old thatched chapel of Raheen was erected in 1729, the site having been granted by the Protestant Baldwin family, after Mr. Baldwin had witnessed a gathering of poor people for Mass in a deep pit, named thereafter, the Mass Pit.

The thatched chapel was used up to 1860. This humble structure was replaced by the present substantial church. The blue stone used in the building of St. Fintan's was brought by horse and cart from a quarry at Newtown, Ballyroan, Co. Laois.

The church was built 1857-1860. In 1857 Fr. Thomas Hennessy was pastor, and he was succeeded in 1859 by Fr. James O'Beirne. The tall windows which are only one foot in width and about 10ft. high are an unusual feature.

In 1979, work was undertaken by local contractor P.J. Grant which included restoring the porch and church sacristy, lowering of the ceiling, erection of new doors and installation of new eve gutters, down pipes, and windows. A car park was also added.

On the 15th December 1985, Bishop Patrick Lennon blessed St. Fintan's following further major refurbishment. Mr. Wilfrid Cantwell was the architect for both phases. Mr. Martin Breen of Shanahoe was contracted to complete this interior renovation (1985) and further refurbishment in 1998.

St. Fintan's Church, Raheen

St. Brigid's, Shanahoe

DATE OF CHURCH: 1968
BUILDING PASTOR: FR. WILLIAM MAHON P.P.
ARCHITECT: S. C. SHESGREEN
BUILDER: CHARLES BREEN
COST: £33,000

SHANAHOE, (SEAN CHUADH, OLD HOLLOW. CUADH OR CUACH IS
LITERALLY A CUP; TOPOGRAPHICALLY A CUP-LIKE HOLLOW,
COMMONLY BETWEEN TWO HILLS).

THE PILGRIM PRIEST, Fr. Benjamin Broughall, was
responsible for the building of the 1816 church. At the
consecration of that church, the local landlord and
donor of the site, Mr. Bourden, of Springmount House,
presented to the people of Shanahoe a painting depicting
St. Peter with the Keys of the Kingdom. This painting had been
presented to him in gratitude for his kindness by a man known
as the *Ditreabhach* (a man
without a tribe).

The picture has been placed on loan
with Abbeyleix Heritage Centre since
1998 and a copy hangs in the new
church.

John Keegan, native of Killeaney, near
Shanahoe, wrote many tales and
poems depicting rural life as he knew
it in the first half of the nineteenth
century and his written accounts are
treasured in the Shanahoe area.
He died in 1849, aged 33.

The Ditreabhach's legacy.

The 1816 church was demolished in 1966 and a new building
of modern design was raised on the site. The foundation stone
was blessed 1st February
1967 by the Auxiliary
Bishop Patrick Lennon.

St. Brigid's, Shanahoe

Parish of Mountrath

CLERGY IN THE PARISH IN THE YEAR 2000
V. REV. LAURENCE T. NEWMAN P.P.
REV. JOHN O'BRIEN C.C.

CATHOLIC POPULATION: 2,100

St. Fintan's Church, Mountrath

> DATE OF CHURCH: 1867
> ARCHITECT: JOHN S. BUTLER
> BUILDERS: BEARWOOD & JOHN RAFTER (ROSENALLIS)
> COST: £ 6,354

MOUNTRATH (*MAIGHEAN RÁTHA, THE PLACE OF THE FORT*).

IN THE LATE 1700'S, the place of worship used by the parishioners was a chapel at a place called "The Brook", on a sandbank in a tributary of the River Nore. About 1794, Bishop Daniel Delany, seeking to build a proper church, finally obtained a site from Mr. Hawkesworth, agent for Lord Castlecoote, who afterwards managed to procure a lease 'for ever', from his employer. Work began about 1795, and the parishioners, shocked by the site's dimensions, called it "Delany's Folly".

The foundations of Dr. Delany's church were defective, and Rev. James Dunne P.P. restarted work soon after his appointment in 1857. Ten years later the church of St. Fintan was completed. He was greatly assisted by Brother John Delaney of the Mountrath monastery of St. Patrick, who travelled to North America, Australia, New Zealand, and California, to raise funds for the building of the church, raising over £4,000. Dr. Comerford describes St. Fintan's as "one of the finest parochial churches in the Diocese". The church is of fine neo-Gothic style, with load-bearing masonry walls which are faced with a limestone ashlar. The exterior finishes are in limestone ashlar with certain details in sandstone, and the interior, in general, is a mixture of plasterwork with columns, also in cream sandstone.

The foundation stone was laid on the 17th February 1861, Feast Day of St. Fintan, patron saint of Clonenagh parish. The ceremony was performed by Bishop James Walshe.

Bishop Daniel Delany (1788 - 1814) was born in 1747 in the townland of Paddock, two miles from Mountrath. In his lifetime he built the fine parish church in Tullow and founded the Brigidine Sisters and Patrician Brothers.

St. Fintan's Church, Mountrath

John Duffy

Mrs Hawkesworth, wife of the Mr. Hawkesworth earlier mentioned, converted to Catholicism in her last illness. Her home, which later became part of the Convent, was the Orange Lodge of Mountrath, at the turbulent time of the church's foundation.

Fr. Philip Connolly from Co. Monaghan was ordained in 1814, and served in Carlow, Rathvilly, Dublin, and Mountrath. In 1819, he applied to Dr. Slater, Vicar-Apostolic for New Holland and Van Diemen's land, for work among the convicts and the Catholic Settlers in Australia. He became Australia's first permanently - appointed priest, (along with Fr. John Joseph Therry), and later became the first Vicar-General of Australia.

Sacred Heart, The Hollow

DATE OF CHURCH: 1887
STYLE: ROMANESQUE
ARCHITECT: WILLIAM HAGUE
BUILDER: WILLIAM EGAN, MOUNTMELLICK
BUILDING PASTOR: FR. EDWARD BRENNAN P.P.

AT THE END OF THE PENAL TIMES, a thatched chapel served the people of this locality. It was administered by Fr. Quigley, a friar.

Bishop James Lynch dedicated the Sacred Heart Church in December 1887.

Work was carried out to re-order the church in 1983-1984, and it was re-opened on the third Sunday after Easter 1984. Architect was Michael Crowe, Dublin; contractor was Michael Regan, Graiguecullen, Carlow; artist employed was Ray Carroll, of Dublin. The re-ordering cost £34,000.

In December 1987, as his first official act as Bishop, Bishop Laurence Ryan celebrated Mass for the centenary of the church.

Sacred Heart, The Hollow

Parish of Ballyfin

PARISH PRIEST IN THE YEAR 2000
V. REV. PATRICK DUNNY P.P.

CATHOLIC POPULATION: 1,300

St. Fintan's Church, Ballyfin

> DATE OF CHURCH: C. 1820
> BUILDING PASTOR: FR. CHRISTOPHER DOYLE C.C.

BALLYFIN (*BAILE FIONN, FIONN, FINNE*, FAIR, BRIGHT; THE BRIGHT TOWN).

PRIOR TO 1823, Ballyfin was part of the parish of Clonenagh. St. Fintan's monastery of Clonenagh had seven churches and two or three of these were in the Ballyfin area. In that year it was formed into a separate curacy and, in 1847, became a parish in its own right.

Ballyfin was once part of the demesne lands of the O'Mores, chieftains of Leix. In reward for his services against the O'Mores, Patrick Crosbie was granted their estates. Following a later confiscation of the estate from his great-grandson, the demesne was granted to Piriam Pole of Shute, Devonshire. In 1812, Sir Charles Coote purchased the estate from the Poles. It was he who built the neo-classical mansion which replaced Pole's house of 1778. In 1930, the great house and lands were purchased by the Patrician Brothers as a College.

The present St. Fintan's is the third church to occupy the site. Previous churches dated from c. 1714 and 1774. An extant inscribed stone slab confirms the latter. In 1975-1976 the church was greatly renovated, under Fr. James Moran, with alterations to the sanctuary, the removal of the gallery and the addition of the porch. In 1993 a new car park with tennis courts was erected with the assistance of a F.Á.S. scheme. In 2000, Fr. Patrick Dunny had a new stained glass window installed, depicting the Logo of Jubilee Year 2000 A.D.

St. Fintan's Church, Ballyfin

John Duffy

PORTARLINGTON DEANERY

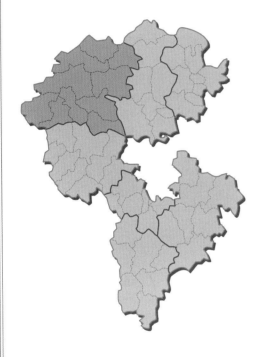

PARISHES

PORTARLINGTON	76, 77
EMO	78, 79
MOUNTMELLICK	80, 81
ROSENALLIS	82
CLONASLEE	83
KILLEIGH	84, 85
CLONBULLOGUE	86, 87
EDENDERRY	88, 89
RHODE	90, 91
DAINGEAN	92, 93, 94

Parish of Portarlington

CLERGY IN THE PARISH IN THE YEAR 2000
V. REV. MICHAEL NOONAN P.P.
REV. THOMAS O'BYRNE C.C.

CATHOLIC POPULATION: 5,000

St. Michael's Church, Portarlington

DATE OF CHURCH: 1842
BUILDING PASTOR: FR. TERENCE O'CONNELL P.P.

PORTARLINGTON (*CÚL AN TSÚDAIRE*,
THE RECESS OF THE TANNER).

THE TOWN was founded in 1666 by Sir Henry Bennet, Home Secretary to Charles II, to whom the King made a grant of the lands of O'Dempsey, Viscount Clanmalier, forfeited in 1641. Sir Henry Bennet was created Baron Arlington. He obtained a Charter, creating a Borough within part of the lands of Cooletoodera, and introduced English settlers. The Parliament of Orrery and Ormond enacted that English names replace the Irish names of places, so the Borough of Cooletoodera received the name of Port-Arlington, or Arlington's Fort.

Fr. Terence O'Connell, P.P acquired the leases of the lands for the new Church site. He had previously been Administrator in Carlow and worked on the large project of the erection of Carlow Cathedral.

The stones used in the building of the church came from the bed of the

Fr. Terence O'Connell, P. Builder of Churches at Portarlington, Emo and Killenard.

canal being constructed between Portarlington and Monastervin. Fr. Edward O'Leary extended the church by 20 feet in 1915 and added chancel, side chapels, nuns' choir, the sacristies and baptistry. He completed Canon John O'Hanlon's "The History of the Queen's County"; Canon O'Hanlon died in 1905 and the two volume work appeared in 1907 and 1914.

A plaque in the side porch commemorates Fr. Terence O'Connell, P.P., who built the churches of Portarlington, Killenard and Emo, and who brought the Presentation Nuns (1854) and the Christian Brothers (1863) to Portarlington. Following his death in 1875 the parish was divided, with Emo and Rath becoming a new parish. Fr. O'Connell is interred in the parish church, as is his successor, Fr. Hugh Mahon P.P. (1875-1889).

In 1971, under architect Wilfrid Cantwell, the church of St. Michael's was refurbished in accordance with Vatican II.

St. Michael's Church, Portarlington

St. John's Church, Killenard

DATE OF CHURCH: 1835
BUILDING PASTORS: FRS. JOHN DUNNE
AND TERENCE O'CONNELL
STYLE: CRUCIFORM

KILLENARD (*CILL AN ÁIRD*, CHURCH ON THE HEIGHT).

THE AREA OF LEY, OR LEIGHE, was one of the seven territories comprising the ancient Offalia. The castle of Ley which was situated in this district, changed hands numerous times in conflicts down through the centuries.

The first church was built here in 1735, the site given by Mr. Smith of Mount Henry who, tradition says, saw his housekeeper setting out for Treascon where the locals gathered secretly for Mass. The old church stood in the present graveyard. St. John's Church was begun by Fr. John Dunne P.P. - the walls were 5ft. high when he died in 1832. Construction was completed under Fr. O'Connell P.P. The church is of simple cruciform style with a classical front, which was added by Fr. E. O'Leary.

The church is adorned with statues placed in the front wall, to St. Patrick & St. Brigid, with a statue of St. John over the entrance. Two wall plaques state the dates of construction and renovation to be 1835 and 1907. A plaque over the doorway, in Irish, says "Church of St. John the Evangelist".

The choir rail and round seat is dated 1915; the paschal candlestick - 1921; the silver sanctuary lamp holder - 1933. The monstrance has the inscription "The Confraternity of Portarlington 1797", and a new set of stations were erected in 1925 at a cost of £100.

The church was refurbished in 1970-1975 under architect Wilfrid Cantwell.

St. John's Church, Killenard

Parish of Emo

CLERGY IN THE PARISH IN THE YEAR 2000
V. REV. JOHN WALSH P.P.
REV. JOHN McEVOY

CATHOLIC POPULATION: 1,300

St. Paul's Church, Emo

DATE OF CHURCH: 1862
ARCHITECT: J. S. BUTLER
STYLE: GOTHIC REVIVAL
BUILDING PASTOR: FR. TERENCE O'CONNELL

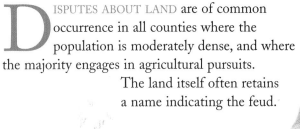

Monument to Aline, Countess of Portarlington

EMO; *IOMA*, CONTENTION, CONFLICT.

DISPUTES ABOUT LAND are of common occurrence in all counties where the population is moderately dense, and where the majority engages in agricultural pursuits. The land itself often retains a name indicating the feud.

Coolbanagher Castle was a dependency of Dunamase. In the 1500's, the area came into the possession of Robert Hartpole, after the Irish clans had been expelled from the Queen's County.

The site for St. Paul's was donated by Lord Portarlington, and the church was built during the pastorate of Fr. Terence O'Connell P.P., mainly by the exertions of the resident curate, Fr. William Hooney. On the death of Fr. O'Connell in 1875, the P.P. of the new parish of Emo was Fr. John Phelan. The bell tower was added during his pastorate. At the entrance of the church is a statue of St. Paul, patron saint of the church. Stained glass windows of great beauty adorn the building.

The church was refurbished in 1963 by Fr. P.A. Maher P.P., when it was reroofed and the inside walls studded.

The Earl of Portarlington erected a monument in the church to his wife Aline, Countess of Portarlington. It is the work of the sculptor Boehm, reputed to be one of his finest works, and is a recumbent effigy in Carrara marble. Countess Aline, who resided at Emo Park, was a convert to Catholicism from 1867 and died in 1874. Her grave is positioned near the Passionist Mission Cross.

St. Paul's Church, Emo

John Duffy

Church of the Sacred Heart, Rath

Church of the Sacred Heart, Rath

DATE OF CHURCH: 1877
STYLE: GOTHIC
BUILDING PASTOR: FR. JOHN PHELAN P.P.
COST: £3,000

RATH (*RATH*, RATH OR FORT).

ON THE DEATH OF FR. TERENCE O'CONNELL P.P., Portarlington, in 1875, the old parish of Courtwood was united with that of Emo as a new Parish. Following the erection of the church at Emo it was decided to replace the wooden structure at Courtwood.

The site was donated by Mr. E. Dease M.P. of Rath House, Ballybrittas, who also gave a generous donation.
The parishioners held a meeting and decided to tax themselves 10s in the pound of their valuation towards a building fund, thereby raising £1,400. Fr. John Phelan, the new P.P., gave £100. The church was built in 1877, in the Gothic style.
Blue limestone from a quarry near The Heath was used.
The church is 95ft. by 58ft. divided into a nave and aisles, these being separated by ornamental pillars resting on cut stone pedestals. Stone for this section came from Stradbally and Bagenalstown. The entrance is of rich design with granite moulding. As in 'modern' design of the period, galleries were dispensed with. Bishop James Walsh performed the opening ceremony on 25th August 1880, attended by 4,000 people. The local choir, lead by Mrs. Dease, was assisted by the girls from the orphanage in Stradbally.

In 1950, the bell tower was struck by lightning and fell to the ground. The church was then reroofed. In 1990 a Lourdes Grotto was erected in the church grounds.

Parish of Mountmellick

CLERGY IN THE PARISH IN THE YEAR 2000
V. REV. FRANCIS MacNAMARA P.P, V.F.
REV. PATRICK HENNESSY C.C,
REV. JOSEPH WHITTLE S.D.B., C.C.

CATHOLIC POPULATION: 4,400

St. Joseph's Church, Mountmellick

DATE OF CHURCH: 1878
ARCHITECT: J.J. McCARTHY
COST: £ 6,555
BUILDING PASTOR: FR. THOMAS MURPHY P.P.

MOUNTMELLICK (*MOÍNTEACH MILEACH*; *MONTIAGHE*, MARSH, A BOGGY PLACE; MELLICK, LOW MARSHY GROUND).

THE TOWN OF MOUNTMELLICK is of quite 'recent' origin, as it does not appear on the map of Leix and Offaly, made c. 1563. Mountmellick became a distinct parish in 1770. In 1776 the town had 508 Catholics. In earlier times Derryguile had a Mass pit. Prior to the present church, Portnahinch and Ivy Chapel had a church and graveyard while Kilmainham had a still earlier church. Before the building of St. Joseph's, a church in Graigue was in use from 1812.
In 1833, the third parish priest of Mountmellick was appointed. He was Rev. Andrew Healy, who introduced the Presentation Sisters in 1854. He was succeeded in 1864 by Rev. Thomas Murphy. Fr. Murphy was responsible for building St. Joseph's church beside the convent.

The site for St Joseph's was acquired from the Marquis of Drogheda, with a lease for ever. The first Mass was celebrated there in July 1878. The church is a fine example of the Gothic style championed by architects Pugin and McCarthy in the 19th century, and is built of cut limestone. In 1912 the church tower was erected. In 1965, the church was much enlarged when it was converted from rectangular shape to cruciform by the addition of a transept, sanctuary, sacristies, and boiler house. The transept measures 86ft by 37ft., and the sanctuary is 30ft. in depth. The architect was J.R. Boyd Barrett, and the builder was Sweeney of Portarlington. Cost was £100,000. A new electronic organ was installed in 1998.

Bishop Patrick Lennon was P.P. of Mountmellick 1966-1967.

St. Joseph's Church, Mountmellick

St. Mary's Church, Clonaghadoo

DATE OF CHURCH: 1970
ARCHITECT: J.R. BOYD BARRETT
BUILDER: CHARLES BREEN
BUILDING PASTOR: FR. CORNELIUS CROWLEY P.P.
COST: £ 38,000
SEATING: 450

CLONAGHADOO (*CLUAIN*, MEADOW, LEVEL AREA; *EACH*, A STEED, HORSE; *DUBH*, BLACK. MEADOW OF THE BLACK HORSE).

IN 1770, Fr. Thady Duane had a church at Clonaghadoo and, after celebrating Mass there, would walk to Mountmellick to celebrate Mass in a private house. He was uncle of Fr. Anthony Duane, builder of the old church at Graigue.

Beside the remains of the castle in Castlebrack are the walls of an old church, which appears on McGeoghegan's list of parochial churches of the early 1600's. An adjoining graveyard has headstones dating from 1721

The modern church replaced an earlier building dating from 1825, which in turn, had replaced a humble thatched structure built c. 1777. The old church was in poor condition and it was decided in 1967 that a new church should be built. The church is of modern design featuring large areas of stained glass. The walls are faced with rough cast plaster with smooth cement bands topped by a turret bearing a bronze cross. The roof structure is of steel. The church was blessed by Bishop Patrick Lennon on 17th March 1970. From the old church came the altar, tabernacle, and the free standing bell.

In 1999-2000 a major refurbishment was carried out. A new roof was added and the sanctuary was re-designed with a very pleasing result.

St. Mary's Church, Clonaghadoo

John Duffy

Parish of Rosenallis

PARISH PRIEST IN THE YEAR 2000
V. REV. THOMAS WALSHE P.P.

CATHOLIC POPULATION: 1,200

St. Brigid's Church, Rosenallis

> DATE OF CHURCH: 1976
> BUILDING PASTOR: FR. TOM DONOHOE P.P.
> ARCHITECT: J.R. BOYD BARRETT
> BUILDER: CHARLES BREEN

ROSENALLIS (*ROS FIONNGHLAISE*, THE WOOD OF THE CLEAR STREAM. *ROS*, PROMONTORY, HEADLAND; *FIONN*, FAIR; *GLAISE*, STREAMLET).

THIS PARISH covered the entire Barony of Tinnahinch until the formation of the parishes of Mountmellick and Clonaslee in the late 1700's, and was dedicated to St. Brigid. In 1302, Oregan (Uí Riagain), or Rosenallis, was granted to the Knights Hospitallars of St. John of Jerusalem, a nursing order, who stayed until the suppression of the monasteries by Henry VIII, in 1537. In the 1500's the monastery was destroyed but was repaired and used as a parochial church during the next century until the war of 1641-1654, when the O'Dunne territory was decimated by Cromwell's troops.

Rosenallis village was established as a Quaker settlement in the mid-17th century by the first members of the Society of Friends to settle in Ireland. They had a major influence on the development of the area for the next 200 years. Their burial ground remains at the outskirts of the village.

About 1690 a Williamite contingent was quartered near Rosenallis. The Catholics were allowed by the Protestant landlord, Robert Pigott, to build a Mass House at Rushin. About 1714, another Mass House was built, the foundations of which were unearthed in 1900 on the farm of Andrew Gorman. In 1792, a small chapel of stone and lime with a thatched roof was built on Mr. Pigott's land. This chapel functioned until 1859 when a new church was built, with Mr. Pigott of Capard contributing £200 towards the total cost of £600. This church was demolished 117 years later when a modern church was built on the site of the old parish hall in Rosenallis. This church was consecrated by Bishop Patrick Lennon in 1976.

The Millennium was marked by the installation of a new pine ceiling in 1999 and a new Stone Carpet in 2000.

St. Brigid's Church, Rosenallis

John Duffy

Parish of Clonaslee

PARISH PRIEST IN THE YEAR 2000
V. REV. JAMES K. GAHAN P.P.
CATHOLIC POPULATION: 1,300

St. Manman's Church, Clonaslee

> DATE OF CHURCH: 1813
> BUILDING PASTOR: FR. THADY DUNNE P.P.

CLONASLEE (*CLUAIN NA SLÍ,* THE MEADOW BY THE WAY).

THIS DISTRICT was ruled by the O'Dunnes, who had their stronghold at Brittas. The Barony of Tinnahinch was initially a single parish. In 1770, Mountmellick became a separate parish; in 1793, Clonaslee and Rosenallis separated but re-joined in 1811, when they formed a parish until another final separation in 1828. Clonaslee now contains Kilmanman, and this is the more ancient parish name, after St. Manman who founded a church here in the 7th century.

In 1771, Squire Francis O'Dunne, head of the O'Dunne family, conformed to the Established Faith (possibly to hold on to his lands) and this probably accounts for the move of the Catholic place of worship to the village of Clonaslee in that year. This was a humble thatched structure and occupied a site close to the present stone church which replaced it in 1813. A foundation stone over the entrance door states, "This chapel was erected Anno Dom 1813. The Rev. Thaddaeus Dunne Pastor". This Fr. Thaddaeus Dunne had been P.P. of Rosenallis since 1802 and received charge of the re-united parishes. He was born in 1768 in the locality and was educated in the College des Lombards in Paris. He died in 1828, and is interred at Reary.

The church was built by local tradesmen. The old bell at the rear of the church is dated 1720. The bell at the front was brought from Daingean in 1955. The altars are made of Clonaslee stone and limestone. The main altar was a gift of Fr. John Egan, Los Angeles, native of the parish. The Baptismal font was donated by the Keegan family in memory of their young daughter.

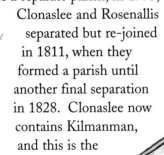

St. Manman's Church, Clonaslee

Parish of Killeigh

CLERGY IN THE PARISH IN THE YEAR 2000
V. REV. JOHN STAPLETON P.P.
RT. REV. MSGR. THOMAS COONAN V.G., C.C.

CATHOLIC POPULATION: 2,900

The Old Church at Killeigh (1808 - 1971)

St. Patrick's Church, Killeigh

DATE OF CHURCH: 1971
ARCHITECT: PATRICK J. SHEHAN
BUILDER: J. J. KILMARTIN
BUILDING PASTOR: FR. DANIEL KENNEDY P.P.
SEATING: 600
COST: £70,000

here is an early Bishop of Kildare, Finn Mac Tiarchan, who died in 1160 A.D.

A convent of Augustinian Nuns also existed in Killeigh. Margaret O'Carroll, mother of a member of the Order, Finola, conducted two large festivals on the Feast Day of St. Senchell, one in Killeigh and one in Rathangan, Co. Kildare.

The waters of Killeigh's Seven Blessed Wells are said to have curative powers.

KILLEIGH (*CILL ACHAIDH*, CHURCH OF THE FIELD; EARLIER *ACHA-DROMA-FADA*, THE FIELD OF THE LONG RIDGE. 'CILL' WAS PREFIXED AFTER ST. SENCHELL HAD HIS CHURCH IN THE AREA. THE LONG RIDGE IS THE PREDOMINANT FEATURE OF THE EXTENSIVE FLAT COUNTRYSIDE).

The church is an irregular octagon in shape, built of brick with plaster dash exterior. On the 12th September, 1971, the foundation stone was blessed by Bishop Patrick Lennon. It replaced an old cruciform church (1808), from which two stone statues were retained.

AT THE BEGINNING OF THE 6TH CENTURY, St. Senchell (the Elder), converted by St. Patrick, founded his monastery at Killeigh. Many ancient local chieftains are buried in the monastery's graveyard. O'Conor Faly built a Franciscan monastery there in 1393. This was on the road to Tullamore. Stone from its walls was later used locally in buildings. Buried

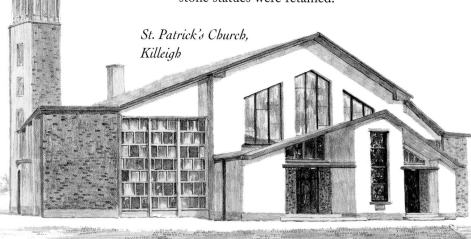

St. Patrick's Church, Killeigh

John Duffy

St. Joseph's Church, Ballinagar

DATE OF CHURCH: 1837
STYLE: GOTHIC, BARN-TYPE
BUILDING PASTOR: FR. JAMES KINSELLA P.P.

BALLINAGAR (BETTER 'BELLANAGAR', BEAL ÁTHA NA GCARR,
THE FORD MOUTH OR FORD OF THE CARS).
THE FORDABLE CROSSING POINTS OF RIVERS WERE KNOWN TO
THE VERY EARLIEST COLONISTS, AND DISTINGUISHED BY NAME.
THIS FORD IS BELIEVED TO HAVE BEEN NEAR BALLINAGAR,
ON THE ROAD TO GEASHILL.

THE BALLINAGAR AREA was served by a thatched chapel in Penal times and the present church was built over it. It has a pinnacled belfry.

The church has a chalice of Fr. James Kinsella, dating from 1847. The *Irish Press* newspaper featured an article on the blessing of the Stations of the Cross by Bishop Thomas Keogh in 1938, with accompanying photograph. The stations had been presented to Fr. Tom Burke, the Dominican preacher, by the Irish Community of New York, "in recognition of his able championing of their cause during a wave of calamitous teaching in America against the Irish Race". The stations have frames of Austrian Oak, and the figures are in relief on a background of leaf gold. Their erection was the occasion of the first official visit to St. Joseph's by Bishop Thomas Keogh.

St. Joseph's Church, Ballinagar

St. Mary's Church, Raheen

St. Mary's Church, Raheen

DATE OF CHURCH: 1935
STYLE: RECTANGULAR
ARCHITECT: P. J. FOLEY, DUBLIN
BUILDING PASTOR: FR. LUKE BYRNE P.P.
COST: £10,000

RAHEEN (LITTLE RATH, FORT).
RAHEEN CASTLE STOOD IN THIS TOWNLAND.

THE AREA OF GEASHILL was the scene of a fierce battle c.500 B.C. The ancient annals record the existence of many mounds in the area where Heber and other chiefs were buried. In the 1800's human bones were unearthed in this locality in large quantities.

St. Mary's replaced an older chapel situated on the opposite side of the road. The cost of the building was kept low by the voluntary assistance of local people in drawing materials, etc. The building project was initiated by Fr Luke Byrne P.P. His tombstone is to the left of the entrance, near the bell. When the church opened in March 1935, the P.P. was Fr. Michael P. Kennedy. Bishop Matthew Cullen officiated at the opening ceremony.

Parish of Clonbullogue

CLERGY IN THE PARISH IN THE YEAR 2000
VERY REV. PATRICK GAYNOR P.P.
REV. PATRICK DUNNE, C.S.SP., C.C.

CATHOLIC POPULATION: 1,400

Church of the Sacred Heart, Clonbullogue

> DATE OF CHURCH: C. 1820
> STYLE: CRUCIFORM

CLONBULLOGUE
(*CLUAIN BULLÓG*, MEADOW OF THE GRAIN).

IN THE NEARBY RUINS of a church in Cloncrane is interred Rev. John Moore, P.P. of Clonbullock, who died in 1793. His chalice is preserved in Sacred Heart Church.

The village of Clonbullogue is in a fertile area surrounded by large tracts of bogland. In 1798 on the Bracknagh road, Wexford rebels Fr. Mogue Kearns and Capt. Anthony Perry were captured and later executed in Edenderry.

The Church of the Sacred Heart is built of limestone and is cruciform in shape, like many of its style from the early 19th century. The front door is now at the rear of the church. In 1983 the building was renovated and the sanctuary reconstructed in keeping with the new liturgy.

St. Brochan's Church, Bracknagh

> DATE OF CHURCH: C. 1845
> STYLE: BARN-TYPE
> BUILDING PASTOR: FR. JOHN DUNNE P.P.

BRACKNAGH (BREACHNACH, A SPECKLED PLACE; OR MORE LIKELY, A REFERENCE TO FARRAN NA BRACHAN, THE TERRITORY OF ST. BROCHAN).

THE LEABHAR CLUAINA SOSTA (Book of Clonsast) was produced in this area. A considerable portion of its contents is preserved in the Royal Irish Academy and is known as the Leabhar Breac, referring to a location near Athlone to which St. Broghan and his monks fled from Clonsast, in the 7th century.

Church of the Sacred Heart, Clonbullogue

Ruins of Ballynowlart Church near Bracknagh

Church of the Immaculate Conception, Walsh Island

St. Brochan's
Church, Bracknagh

DATE OF CHURCH: C. 1824	
STYLE: CRUCIFORM	

In 1798 Mass was said under a tree about 200 yds from Milgrove Bridge. The field was called the Priest's Island. Three priests are interred in the present church, Rev. John Dunne, (d. 1856), who had been parish priest for 32 years; Rev. E. O'Leary, (d. 1850), and the earliest date of interment in the church was March 1845, for Rev. James Murphy, which suggests the early 1840's as time of construction. The church was re-ordered in the 1980's.

The ruins of an old church still stand in the middle of a field in Ballynowlart townsland, on the road from Bracknagh to Rathangan. It is said that c.1650 Cromwell and his troops burned the church, killing those within, since known as the 'Ballynowlart Martyrs'. An excavation in October 1917 unearthed the remains of 108 persons about eighteen inches below the surface. These were re-interred in Bracknagh.

IN BISHOP MACGEOGHEGAN'S list of churches and chapels of Kildare, (early 1600's), Walsh Island is referred to as "Innish", an island. This area, apart from a strip of land which provided passage on the Daingean side through Ballinakill, was surrounded by deep marshy bogs which were not accessible until the Barrow Drainage Scheme was conducted in the 1930's.

Fr. James Breen, curate, was instrumental in having the first National Turf Cutting Competition brought to Monevane, Walsh Island, in 1935. The first sod was cut by President Eamon de Valera. As a result of this event the massive 4,000 acre development of Clonsast Bog began under the Turf Development Board, later to become Bord na Móna.

Ballintemple church, dating from the. 15th century, is one of the oldest structures in Walsh Island.

The church of the Immaculate Conception was built c. 1824, supposedly on the site of an earlier church. It is one of the oldest surviving buildings in the area.

Church of the
Immaculate Conception,
Walsh Island

The church was renovated in the 1970's, when the balcony at the rear and confessionals were removed. Behind the altar is a treasured painting of Mother and Child, which marries Byzantine with Western religious art, the work of an early 20th century Slavonic artist.

Parish of Edenderry

Clergy in the Parish in the year 2000
Rt. Rev. Msgr. John McDonald P.P.
Rev. Laurence Malone C.C.

Catholic Population: 4,200

St. Mary's Church, Edenderry

> Date of Church: 1919
> Style: Hiberno-romanesque
> Architect: William Scott
> Building Pastor: Fr. Paul Murphy P.P.
> Cost: £ 65,000 for Building and
>   Contents to 1929

Edenderry (*Eadan Doirie* the hill brow of the oak woods), from the densely wooded area overlooking the town, the most distinctive feature of the landscape. In the 16th century the place was called Coolestown, after the family of Cooley (or Cawley) who had a castle in the area.
The town of Edenderry was founded by Lord Downshire, (1788 - 1845), who also built Blessington, Co. Wicklow.

Pierce de Bermingham was an early settler who was granted large tracts in this area. In old Gaelic, 'Pierce' was translated Feorais and, after the establishment of a Franciscan monastery in 1325, the name Mainister Mhic Feorais arose, later *Monasteroris*. The monastery was quite substantial, accommodating over 300 students. When the monasteries were suppressed by Henry VIII, the lands were granted to Nicholas Herbert at an annual rent of £4. The old parochial church of Monasteroris was built in the 14th century and stood on the West side of the monastery.

The old parish church at Killane was built in 1816 by Fr. James Colgan P.P. Several items from this church were transferred to the new church of St. Mary's, including stained glass windows, the black marble water fonts, and the high altar which is now in the mortuary chapel. Also in this chapel is a picture of Our Lady of Perpetual Succour, brought from Rome by Fr. John Kinsella P.P. 1882-1905.

Fr. Paul Murphy, builder of St. Mary's

From an earlier chapel at Cokery Lane came a small Celtic Cross and a holy water stoup inscribed M.C. (i.e. Monasteroris Chapel) 1742. Another holy water stoup includes in its inscription the date 12+90.

Fr. Paul Murphy P.P., builder of St. Mary's, also placed clay from all the local cemeteries beneath the communion rails to remind parishioners that they were kneeling on the hallowed dust of their forebears. The church at Killane was demolished in the 1940's.

A foundation stone was laid by Bishop Patrick Foley in 1914. He had turned the first sod a year earlier.
The stone for St Mary's was brought by horse and cart from a quarry near Tullamore by the O'Neill brothers of Clonmullen. The church is a large imposing structure of cut stone.
The architect was William Scott, first Professor of Architecture at the National University of Ireland (Dublin).

A tombstone in the grounds of St. Mary's reads "If you seek a monument look around". This is the headstone of a most remarkable man, Fr. Paul Murphy, a native of Co. Cork and P.P. in Edenderry (1910-1933). The foundation stone was laid in 1914 and Fr. Paul faced into the massive task of finding the money to build the church. The money was raised, and the church paid for during his lifetime
- an outstanding achievement.
He also provided a new Convent
for the Sisters of St. John of God.

Two building contractors worked on the project: William Connolly & Sons until 1916 and from 1918 Jeremiah Coffey Contractors of Midleton, Co. Cork. In June 1919 the sparsely furnished church opened. In the late 1920's the altar, pulpit, altar rails and statues were carved and erected by an Italian firm. Interior design of altar rails and pulpit was by Ashlin and Coleman, Architects.

In 1922, new church benches were installed and a beautiful marble pulpit erected in 1930. (This pulpit has a bust of Fr. Paul Murphy carved on it). In 1932 the church was consecrated by Bishop Matthew Cullen. At that time, this indicated that the church no longer had any debts. Less than six months later, Fr. Murphy died.

St. Mary's was not the only monument left by Fr. Paul. He also undertook to rename the streets of the town and in the case of Blundell St., (his favourite), named it after himself, Fr. Paul Street.

St. Mary's Church, Edenderry

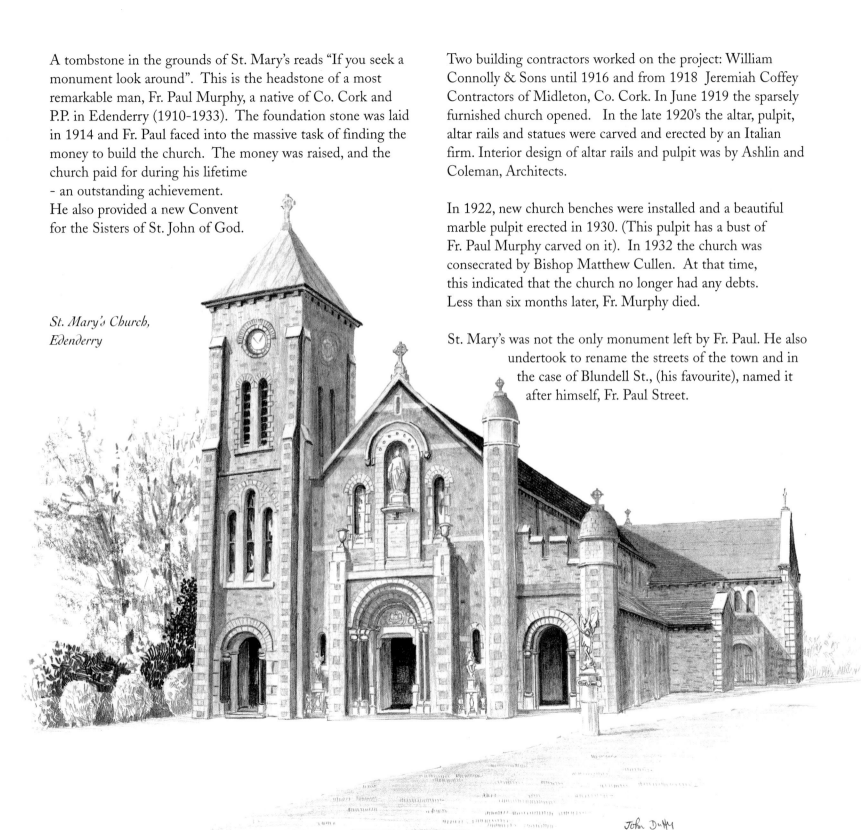

John Duffy

Parish of Rhode

CLERGY IN THE PARISH IN THE YEAR 2000
V. REV. PETER CRIBBIN P.P.
V. REV. EDWARD KELLY (RETIRED CURATE)

CATHOLIC POPULATION: 1,700

St. Peter's Church, Rhode

DATE OF CHURCH: 1816
BUILDING PASTOR: REV. JAMES COLGAN, P.P.
EDENDERRY
RENOVATION ARCHITECTS: W. CANTWELL AND
ASSOCIATES (1970)

RHODE (*RÓD*, ROAD; ANCHORAGE. *TÉAD RÓID*, MOORING ROPE, *CLOCH RÓID*, MOORING STONE / BOLLARD).

IN 1731, in a return made by the Protestant Rector of Primult, John Gibbin, it is stated that Primult had a Mass house since 1714, with one priest officiating. This chapel, or its replacement, was about 40 perches from Rhode on the road to Coolcor. It was used prior to the present church, after which time it functioned as a school.

The site for St. Peter's church in Rhode was a gift of Mr. Thomas Dames, a Protestant from Greenhill. The church is a cruciform building constructed mainly from cut stone with finely-cut limestone and teak mitred windows. It has a slated roof finished with decorative ridge tiles.

(Tradition says that local tradesmen and masons built the church and also worked on later renovations). The foundation stone, located in the boundary wall, is inscribed "St. Peter's chapel, built A.D. 1816 Rev. Js. Colgan P.P." Fr. James Colgan, P.P. Edenderry, died in 1856. After his death, Bishop James Walsh established Rhode and Croghan as a separate parish.

The church has in its possession a chalice of solid silver presented to Rev. Jeremiah Kehoe, P.P. in 1860. There is a fine stained glass window in the Sanctuary depicting St. Peter in chains, dating from c. 1912. The organ (pipe) was purchased in 1992 from the De Vesci Estate in Abbeyleix. The church was renovated and re-roofed in 1959 and the Sanctuary reconstructed in 1970.

St. Peter's Church, Rhode

St. Brigid's Church, Croghan

DATE OF THE CHURCH: 1827
BUILDING PASTOR: REV. JAMES COLGAN, P.P., EDENDERRY
STYLE: CRUCIFORM
RENOVATION ARCHITECTS: W. CANTWELL & ASSOCIATES (1972)

CROGHAN (*CRUACHAN*, A ROUND OR PILED-UP HILL), REFERS TO THE HILL OF CROGHAN, THE MOST CONSPICOUS FEATURE IN THE AREA. IT COMMANDS A MAGNIFICENT VIEW AND, IN ANCIENT TIMES, WAS IN THE TERRITORY OF THE O 'CONNORS FALY, WHOSE CASTLE STOOD ON THE SOUTHWEST. LEGEND STATES THAT THE HILL WAS ALSO VISITED BY ST. PATRICK. A HOLY WELL THERE BEARS HIS NAME.

PRIOR TO THE CONSTRUCTION OF ST. BRIGID'S CHURCH, Mass was celebrated for several years in a barn belonging to Mr. Jonathan Dames. Croghan Church is constructed from cut stone with teak mitred windows and slated roof with decorative ridge tiles. It resembles Rhode Church but is smaller. Reconstruction work was carried out in 1960.

The Sanctuary was reconstructed in 1972.

The chalice still in use in St. Brigid's is of solid silver and was presented to Rev. Jeremiah Kehoe P.P. in 1859.

Of special significance is the Irish Exhibition Altar in carved Oak and walnut manufactured by C. Bull of 21 Suffolk St., Dublin. It was enthusiastically reviewed in The Freeman's Journal in April 1908.

Exhibition Altar

St. Brigid's Church, Croghan

Parish of Daingean

CLERGY IN THE PARISH IN THE YEAR 2000
V. REV. PATRICK O'BYRNE P.P.
V. REV. RICHARD KELLY P.E., C.C.

CATHOLIC POPULATION: 2,700

Mary Mother of God, Daingean

DATE OF CHURCH: 1960
ARCHITECT: J. R. BOYD-BARRETT
BUILDING PASTOR: FR. EDWARD KINSELLA P.P.
SEATING: 850
COST: £60,000

New Church with the Old Church of St. Philip Neri

DAINGEAN, DANGAN, A FORTRESS. PREVIOUSLY, PHILIPSTOWN.

IN OLD MAPS the fortress of Philipstown is called the Fort of Faly. An Act of Parliament 1556 in the Reign King Philip and Queen Mary decreed that the Fort of Ophaly be henceforth called Philipstown.

Fr. Matthew O'Reilly was P.P. 1805-1825 and built a parish church at Philipstown. A replacement church was built by Dr. Denis Kane in 1867 and dedicated to St. Philip Neri, founder of the Oratorians. Dr. Kane was a friend of Cardinal Newman, an Oratorian.

The present church of Mary, Mother of God is an impressive building constructed in Neo-Gothic style. It was built by Turley Builders, Portarlington. Due to the wetness of the site, the foundations had to be very substantial. The building has concrete block walls faced with rustic red brick. The tower, with its impressive copper spire, rises to 110ft.

On 13th August, 2000 Fr. Gregory Corcoran was ordained in this church.

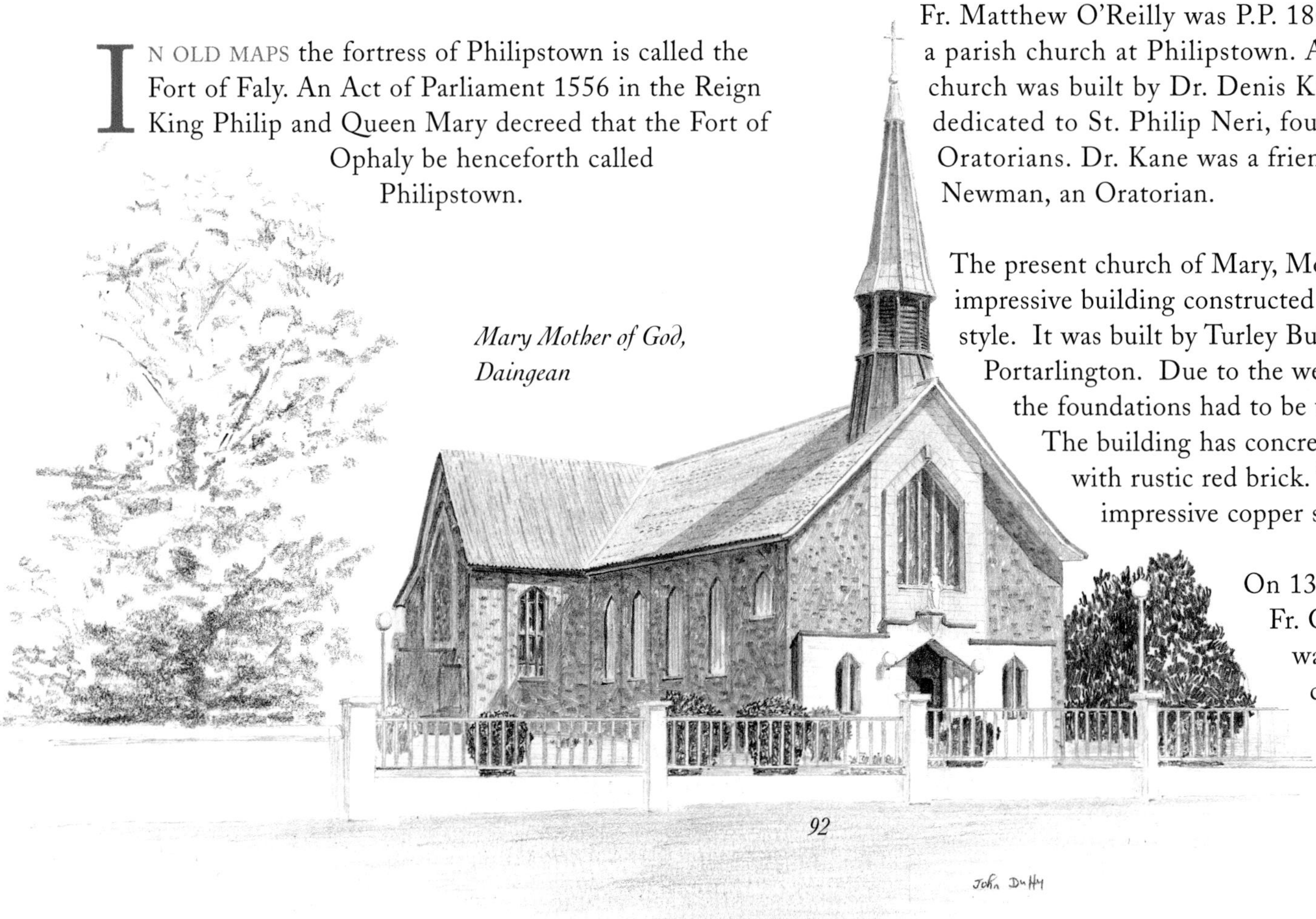

Mary Mother of God, Daingean

John Duffy

St. Coleman's Church,
Kilclonfert

St. Coleman's Church, Kilclonfert

DATE OF CHURCH: 1783
STYLE: CRUCIFORM

KILCLONFERT (*CILL CHLUAINFEARTA*, CHURCH OF THE MEADOW OF THE GROVE. A MORE ANCIENT NAME IS CLUAINFERTA - MUGAINE, MENTIONED IN THE FEILIRE AENGUIS AS IN UÍ FAILGHE).

THE NAME 'KILCLONFERT' indicates a monastic past. The patron saint is St. Coleman whose feast day is celebrated September 3rd.

The church is remarkable for both its age and quality of construction. The architectural historian, William Garner, stated it to be an exceptional survival being a simple cruciform structure with rendered walls, round-headed windows and a two-stage tower with raised coigns. Striking features of the church are the carved stone heads. On each wall of the tower are angelic and animal heads representing the four evangelists: Matthew (man); Mark (lion); Luke (ox). and John (eagle). Above the door is a winged angel and a crucifixion panel, and on the front walls are depictions of St. Peter and St. Paul, to whom the church is dedicated.

Following restoration work in 1934, the church was re-dedicated by Bishop Matthew Cullen. Further renovation was conducted in 1984 under Fr. Kieran O'Byrne P.P. The architect was Mr. Eamon Hedderman. The newly constructed altar provides an immediate focal point in the church.

Stone carvings of the
Church's Patron Saints, Peter and Paul

St. Brigid's Church, Ballycommon

St. Brigid's Church, Ballycommon

DATE OF CHURCH: 1846
BUILDING PASTOR: FR. PATRICK RIGNEY P.P.
STYLE: RECTANGULAR

BALLYCOMMON (*BAILE UI COMAIN*, O'COMMON'S TOWN).

D R COMERFORD states that the site of the old parochial church came to be occupied by a Protestant church, and that all trace of the ancient church had disappeared. (1880's)

In Dr. Mac Geoghegan's listing of churches conducted in the early 1600's he notes that St. Brigid is Patron of the area.

The present church, situated by the canal, has a gallery at its rear. In a renovation and re-ordering of the church, the sacristy area was slightly enlarged and the gallery reduced in size.

Oratory of The Immaculate Conception, Cappincur

CAPPINCUR (CEAPACH AN CHURRAIG, THE TILLAGE PLOT OF THE MARSH). IT IS SPELT 'KEAPANCURRAGH' IN AN INQUISITION OF JAMES I.

D R. COMERFORD states that the place had a grave yard and 'some small portion of a ruin'. The Oratory at Cappincur was originally built as a local hall; Mass was provided there on Sunday mornings. In 1989-1990 it was converted into a permanent Oratory. Cappincur is situated on the edge of Tullamore town.

Oratory of The Immaculate Conception, Cappincur

KILDARE DEANERY

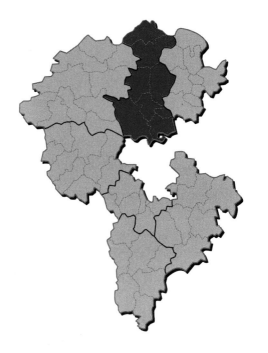

PARISHES

KILDARE   96, 97
CURRAGH CAMP   100
SUNCROFT   101
MONASTEREVIN   102, 103
ALLEN   104, 105
CARBURY   106, 107
BALYNA   108, 109
RATHANGAN   110

SPECIALLY FEATURED

Early History of
the Diocese of Kildare   98
Kildare Cathedral (Church of Ireland) 99

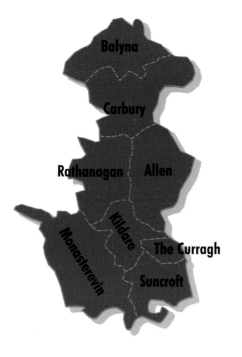

Parish of Kildare

CLERGY IN THE PARISH IN THE YEAR 2000
V. REV. ADRIAN CARBERY P.P.
REV. MICHAEL KANE S.P.S., C.C.

CATHOLIC POPULATION: 5,200

St. Brigid's Church, Kildare

DATE OF CHURCH: 1833, 1851 (SPIRE)
BUILDING PASTOR: FR. PATRICK BRENNAN P.P.
RENOVATION: 1969-1970; EXTENSION: 1974-1975
RENOVATION & EXTENSION ARCHITECT: RICHARD HURLEY
COST OF RENOVATION: £33,000
COST OF EXTENSION: £130,000

KILDARE (*CILL DARA*, CHURCH OF THE OAK)

KILDARE was an English stronghold from the early days of the Norman invasion. The district was granted to De Vesci, who built a castle there. In 1307 the O'Conors had the castle taken from them by Lord Offaly. John Wogan, the Justiciary, took possession, and granted the castle and town of Kildare to John Fitzgerald.

The Carmelite (1290) and Franciscan Orders (1260) were established in Kildare by De Vesci. The Franciscan monastery was at the south side

St. Brigid's Church, Kildare

of the town and they remained at Kildare till the early 18th century.

In 1539 the Franciscan and Carmelite friaries were dissolved by Henry VIII and their communities dispersed. The first bishop of the Reformed Church was appointed in 1540.

The Carlow Morning Post reported on the dedication of the church in 1833 and described the attendance of The Liberator, Daniel O'Connell. He received Communion and afterwards breakfasted at the Presentation Convent. Catholic Emancipation had been achieved in 1829, largely through the agitation of O'Connell and James Warren Doyle (J.K.L.), Bishop of Kildare and Leighlin.

Daniel O'Connell
(1775-1847)

On Tuesday, 5th October 1886, Fr. James B. Kavanagh P.P. was killed in St. Brigid's church by the fall of a marble statue from the altar which struck him on the head. He was a staunch supporter of land reform and it was his belief that each tenant farmer should own one's own holding.

In 1969-1970 under Fr. Peadar Mac Suibhne the church was re-roofed, the gallery removed, a Blessed Sacrament chapel added, and the church adapted to the modern liturgy.

In 1974-1975 a more extensive re-ordering of the church was carried out under Fr. Robert Prendergast. A major extension was built onto the South-facing wall, providing a T-shaped worship space around a free-standing octagonal sanctuary. The altar is made of eight large blocks of granite arranged in a St. Brigid's Cross on each of the four faces. The ambo, Baptismal font and tabernacle pedestal were sculpted in granite by Ray Carroll. Metalwork and enamels are by Patrick McElroy and the stained glass is by Patrick Pye. The Madonna statue is by Oisin Kelly; Penal Cross and Holy Family plaque by Benedict Tutty; the plaster Madonna & Child is by Nel Murphy. The Welcoming Hands on the main doors are the work of Imogen Stuart.

The Carmelite Church, White Abbey, Kildare

DATE OF CHURCH: 1884
STYLE: CRUCIFORM
ARCHITECT: WILLIAM HAGUE
BUILDER: JOHN HARRIS, MONASTEREVAN
COST: £3,500

DE VESCI, who brought the Franciscans to Kildare where they established the Grey Abbey, brought the Carmelite Friars to the town in 1290. They thrived until the reign of Henry VIII when the White Abbey was seized in 1539. For the next 200 years the Friars remained in the area, operating illegally. They returned in the 1750's and erected a church and school close to their old site. This church remained in use for over 100 years until the present church was built in 1884. The builder used Wicklow Granite and local stone from Boston, Rathangan. The church has a tapering spire which rises to 140ft.

On the north transept wall are stone sculptures from the ruins of the Franciscan Grey Abbey. They are similar to the carvings from Great Connell and Dunfierth, both in Kildare, and are probably by the same hand. Of the beautiful stained-glass windows the Rose Window is of special interest, with a central representation of the prophet Elijah, regarded as spiritual father of the Carmelites.

The Carmelite Church, White Abbey, Kildare

EARLY HISTORY OF THE DIOCESE OF KILDARE

St. Brigid's Cross

KILDARE DIOCESE owes its origin to the development from about the year 470 of a monastic complex at Kildare (Church of the Oak Tree) associated with the figure of St. Brigid, the second national patron. Brigid of Kildare worked closely with St. Conleth, a monk from Old Connell near modern Newbridge. Conleth is regarded as the first bishop of Kildare. His consecration is dated about 490. Conleth was a skilled worker in precious metals. The Four Masters record that he died on 3rd May 519. His feast as patron of Kildare diocese is celebrated on 4th May. After his death a monastery of men also developed at Kildare. A succession of abbots also functioned as bishops. The monastery at Kildare was located in a circular enclosure. A life of St. Brigid written by Cogitosus in the ninth century describes in detail the great Church in Kildare, 'a large high building with the decorated shrines of Brigid and Conleth at either side of the altar'. In 836 the Danes destroyed Kildare by fire and sword and carried away the rich shrines of the two saints.

Killeigh (Co. Offaly) was another famous location in the diocese of Kildare with a prolonged monastic history. St. Senchall, supposedly St. Patrick's first convert, established a monastery there. Later the monastery was known as the Priory of the Holy Cross of Canons Regular of St. Augustine. Killeigh was plundered in 1537.

Finn O'Gorman, abbot of Newry, became bishop of Kildare in the twelfth century. He authored *The Book of Leinster*, a collection of historical tracts, tales, poems and genealogies, for Dermot MacMurrough, king of Leinster.

The Cistercians established an Abbey in Monasterevin (Rosglas) in 1178. St. Evin and St. Abban were associated with an earlier Celtic monastery there from the sixth century. The Cistercian Abbey was dissolved in 1539.

In 1223 Ralph de Bristol succeeded as bishop. He built a new stone Cathedral at Kildare. This Anglo-Norman building was largely destroyed during the rebellion of 1641.

The Dominican, Roche MacGeoghegan, became bishop in 1630. A synod of Dublin Province took place in Portarlington parish (Co. Laois) in 1640, with all dioceses represented except Leighlin. In the penal period in common with most dioceses, Kildare could hardly support a bishop. St Oliver Plunkett as Primate recommended that Rome should amalgamate Kildare with the diocese of Leighlin. In 1678 Pope Bl. Innocent XI gave Leighlin *in commendam* to Mark Forstall O.S.A., already bishop of Kildare since 1676.

KILDARE CATHEDRAL
Church of Ireland

KILDARE received its present name, wrote St Brigid's biographer Cogitosus (Bishop of Kildare in the 10ᵗʰ century) from a mighty oak tree beside which she founded a monastery c. 470.

St. Brigid was born about 453 to a family of noble descent. She received a good education and decided to devote herself to God. She spent time at the church on the Hill of Croghan in Offaly. She established Kildare, her first house being a mere cell, but later a sizeable monastery was erected to cater for a large number of followers. As Abbess, Brigid was assisted by St. Conleth of Old Connell, first Bishop of Kildare. She died in 523 and was buried at Kildare.

The earliest church of St. Brigid and St. Conleth was probably wooden. In 835 it was partially burned down by the Danes who carried off the shrines of the two Saints, although the relics of St. Brigid were preserved.

The cathedral had been plundered 16 times before the Anglo-Norman conquest. In 1132, St. Laurence O'Toole, later Abbot of Glendalough and Archbishop of

Dublin was baptised at Kildare. Ralph de Bristol, Bishop of Kildare, repaired the ruined Cathedral and largely gave the Cathedral its present shape in the years 1223-1230.

The Cathedral was ruinous again by 1600. In the rebellion of 1641 the steeple was beaten down by cannon. During the rebellion, the ornaments, books, and other goods of the Cathedral were taken away by Rosse McGeoghegan, Catholic Bishop of Kildare, who re-consecrated the ancient Cathedral. In 1643, the town was made a garrison stronghold under the Earl of Castlehaven. In 1686 the choir

portion was fitted for Anglican service and restoration work began in 1871. Further restoration was completed in 1996.

The Round Tower (the second on the site) has a base of granite while the remainder is of limestone. It has a fine Romanesque doorway.

With thanks to Dean Robert Townley, Kildare Cathedral – Editor.

Cathedral of St. Brigid, Kildare

Parish of The Curragh

CLERGY IN THE PARISH IN THE YEAR 2000
V. REV. P.J. MCEVOY P.P., S.C.F.
REV. DECLAN FOLEY C.C., C.F.

CATHOLIC POPULATION: 1,400

St. Brigid's, Curragh Camp

DATE OF CHURCH: 1959
ARCHITECT: G. MCNICHOLL & ASSOCIATES
BUILDER: J. DAVIS & CO.
SEATING: 1,400

CURRAGH (*CURRACH*, OR *CORRACH*, USUALLY A MARSH, MOOR. IN THIS CASE, A RACE COURSE. THE CURRAGH OF KILDARE HAS BEEN USED AS A RACE COURSE FROM THE EARLIEST AGES).

IN 1855, Lt. Col. H.W. Lugard was given instructions "for the construction of an infantry camp on the Curragh of Kildare". Work began straightaway on the military camp which was to include churches, hospitals, a library, courthouse and recreational facilities.

The site for the present church was provided by the Minister for Defence. In November 1959, Bishop Thomas Keogh dedicated the building. The church is built of steel portal frames with brick cavity walls and a copper roof.
The teak statue over the entrance, which represents St. Brigid & Children, is by Óisin Kelly. A relic of the True Cross in the church was presented by Fr. Gaspard Rougeot, C.F. The crucifix over the main altar is by Patrick Pye, and the Stations of the Cross are by Imogen Stuart. The stained-glass windows over the entrance are by

Mr. John Murphy, while the Tabernacle is by Brother Benedict Tutty, O.S.B., Glenstal Abbey.

During the year 2000 architect Eamonn Hedderman guided the Parish Pastoral Council in co-operation with the Military Authorities in a major Millennium project - the refurbishment of the Church interior. New wooden sanctuary furnishings were crafted in the military engineering workshops: altar, ambo, seating and chair. The altar is made of American White Oak, using 124 individual ribs. The re-dedication ceremony took place in May 2001.

The Curragh Command is now known as the Defence Forces Training Centre (DFTC), following Army re-structuring.

During World War II the Curragh Camp held a number of German and British prisoners of war. These men often obtained day work outside of the Camp and their employers paid their wages directly to the Camp authorities who issued 'Curragh Coins' to the prisoners. This was an internal commercial system and the coins had value only in the shops of the Camp.

Curragh, World War II coin (actual size)

St. Brigid's, Curragh Camp

Parish of Suncroft

St. Brigid's, Suncroft

DATE OF CHURCH: 1907
STYLE: GOTHIC, RECTANGULAR
ARCHITECT: H. BYRNE , DUBLIN
BUILDERS: P. NOLAN, MONAGHAN
BUILDING PASTOR: FR. WILLIAM RAMSBOTT P.P.

THE HISTORY OF THIS AREA GOES BACK TO PAGAN TIMES AND THE EARLY NAME FOR THIS PLACE IS *BEL ATHA SEANAITH* THE MOUTH OF THE FORD OF SEANATH, HENCE THE OLD NAME OF *BALLYSONAN*. A BATTLE WAS FOUGHT AT *ATH SEANAITH IN 735,* AND IS DOCUMENTED IN THE ANNALS OF CLONMACNOISE.

IN 1650, the fortress of Ballyshannon, held by Pierce Fitzgerald surrendered to Cromwell's commander-in-chief, Col. John Hewson, who described it as follows - "the first or outer moat was 25ft. wide with 12ft of water; the second moat was 40ft. broad. The fortified mount and the church were within the fortress".

The site for the church of St. Brigid was donated to the parish by Mr. Patrick Boland who died in 1871. The church is built of local limestone and comprises nave, sanctuary, side chapel, and two sacristies. The door and window dressings are of granite from Ballyknockan,

Co. Wicklow. The entrance is deeply moulded with heavy polished granite columns to each side. A richly-moulded arch of polished granite columns divides the nave from the sanctuary. The roof is supported by finely-wrought tresses and the ceiling is of pitch pine divided into panels.

In 1992, refurbishment took place when the old altar was removed and a new sacristy installed.

A millennium oak tree was planted in the church grounds on St. Brigid's Day, 2000, and a commemorative stone placed to mark the event. An unusual plaque is mounted on the entrance wall of the church. It reads: "Time Capsule placed here on Confirmation Day March 28 Jubilee Year 2000 by Bishop Laurence Ryan. To be opened in 2050".

TIME CAPSULE
PLACED HERE ON CONFIRMATION DAY
MARCH 28 JUBILEE YEAR 2000
BY BISHOP LAURENCE RYAN
TO BE OPENED IN 2050

St. Brigid's, Suncroft

Parish of Monasterevin

CLERGY IN THE PARISH IN THE YEAR 2000
V. REV. DENIS O'SULLIVAN P.P.
REV. MARK TOWNSEND C.C.
REV. PAUL McNAMEE C.C.

CATHOLIC POPULATION: 5,200

Church of Saints Peter & Paul, Monasterevin

DATE OF THE CHURCH: 1847
ARCHITECT: RICHARD DEANE BUTLER
BUILDING PASTOR: FR. PHILIP HEALY P.P.
STYLE: GOTHIC

MONASTEREVIN (*MAINISTIR EMHÍN,* THE MONASTERY OF ST. EVIN, FOUNDED HERE IN THE 6TH CENTURY).

THE PARISH OF MONASTEREVIN has a well documented history. In the sixth century this place was colonised by St. Evin with a large number of monks from his native Munster. The area was earlier called 'Ros glas', the green wood. The Cistercian Abbey of Rosglas, or de Rosea Valle, was founded in 1189. It prospered until the general suppression of the monasteries by Henry VIII, and it was surrendered in 1539.

Church of Saints Peter & Paul, Monasterevin

Coolatogher and Passlands were previous locations for catholic worship at Monasterevin. The present church was built during the famine years by local labour, using local limestone. It consists of a wide nave without aisles or pillars, and has beautiful stained-glass windows. The architect planned for the two towers to be surmounted with spires, surrounded by four pinnacles each. This work was not completed.

The church was dedicated by Fr. Michael Comerford, P.P., on October 19th, 1879. The sermon was preached by Dr. Patrick F. Moran D.D., Bishop of Ossory (later a Cardinal and Archbishop of Sydney). Fr. Comerford, archaeologist and author of the three-volume history of the Dioceses of Kildare & Leighlin, was parish priest in Monasterevin 1878-1888.

Count John McCormack of Moore Abbey (1925-1937), the famous tenor, was a benefactor of the Church. A Bins organ was installed in May 1984. During the 1994-1996 restoration, new painted Stations of the Cross by Fergus Lyons were installed.

In 1899, a fine Celtic Cross monument was erected in the town to the memory of Fr. Edward Prendergast., a native of the parish. He was curate at Monasterevin in 1798 when charged with complicity in the Rebellion for his ministry to the Catholic rebels at their camp on Barn Hill. He was hanged from a tree beside the River Barrow.

Celtic Cross in honour of Fr. Edward Prendergast

Our Lady of Victories Church, Kildangan

In 1746 Richard O'Reilly was born here. He was to become Coadjutor Bishop of Kildare & Leighlin in 1781, and was afterwards Archbishop of Armagh until his death in 1817.

Sacred Heart Church, Nurney

DATE OF THE CHURCH: C. 1820
BUILDING PASTOR: FR. JOHN ROBINSON P.P.
1810-1822

Our Lady of Victories Church, Kildangan

DATE OF THE CHURCH: 1792
COSTS: COVERED BY THE O'REILLY FAMILY
ENLARGEMENT: 1849

KILDANGAN, *CILL DAINGEAN* (CHURCH OF THE FORTRESS), REFERENCE TO THE LOCAL FITZGERALD CASTLE.

IN A PARLIAMENTARY RETURN OF 1731, Richard Foxcroft, Vicar, states that "in the parish of Kildingan there is no Mass House built, but the Priest of Lackagh says Mass often at the back of an old castle there". A chapel, probably erected after 1731, stood beside the castle. This served until 1792, when the present chapel was built. The site was provided by the O'Reilly family, who also defrayed the building costs. It was considerably enlarged in 1849 by Susan, grandmother of Roderic More O'Ferrall Esq., one-time owner of Kildangan Stud. The O'Reillys also provided the school houses at Kildangan, 1834-1836, at a cost of over 400 pounds. The church tower and bell were added in 1881, by Fr. Michael Comerford.

Kildangan was a Rectory of the Abbey of Great Connell (now Newbridge). Three families successively dominated in this area: Fitzgeralds (builders of the castle), Aylmers and, from 1706, the O'Reillys.

NURNEY (*URNAÍDHE*, A PRAYER HOUSE OR ORATORY).

SITUATED ON AN ELEVATED SITE, Nurney church is in traditional barn-style, with a side porch added later. The site for the church was given by Mr. Laurenceson, the local landlord. He told Fr. Robinson to meet him at Nurney graveyard and he would give him a site. He rode around on his pony while the priest followed him with pegs marking out the site. For many years the floor of the church was gravelled and the faithful knelt upon handkerchiefs. At the back of the church is the ruins of a house where the local curate, Fr. Hyland, lived for a time. He died in 1838.

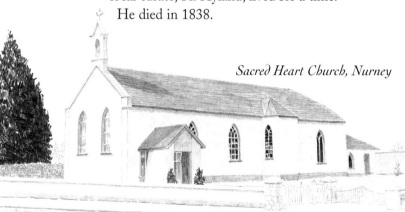

Sacred Heart Church, Nurney

Parish of Allen

CLERGY IN THE PARISH IN THE YEAR 2000
V. REV. EDWARD MOORE P.P.
REV. WILLIAM MURPHY C.C.

CATHOLIC POPULATION: 3,000

Church of the Holy Trinity, Allen

DATE OF CHURCH: 1866-1868
STYLE: GOTHIC REVIVAL
ARCHITECT: JOHN S. BUTLER
BUILDING PASTOR: FR. EUGENE O'REILLY P.P.
COST: £4,000

ALLEN (*ALMHUIN*, THE GREAT NECK) REFERS TO THE HILL OF ALLEN, THE AREA'S PREDOMINANT PHYSICAL FEATURE. THE HILL IS STEEPED IN HISTORY, AND IS BEST KNOWN AS THE RESIDENCE OF FIONN MAC COOL.

TO THE SOUTH WEST OF THE HILL A PATRON DAY was held at a holy well in the townland of Carrick, on the feast of Saints Peter and Paul. The well was dedicated to St. Colman who had resided here.

In Penal times this area was a place of refuge for the prelates of the Diocese of Kildare & Leighlin. Dr. Mark Forstall, first Bishop of Kildare & Leighlin, wrote in 1680: "We are here in a worse plight than before - hardly can we subsist even amongst friends, … I have constructed for myself a hut or thatched hovel, in a marshy wood; … ".
The location of this hovel is thought to be near Kilmeague.

A map of 1752 shows a thatched Mass House in the townland of Grangehiggin. This was replaced by a chapel built in 1783 by Fr. William Lawlor. This chapel was itself replaced by the new church. The Architectural Archives state it to be built during 1866-1868.

The church is built of dressed limestone, and has an octagonal spire atop a square tower. The church was renovated in 1920 and the Sanctuary re-ordered in more recent times.

Church of the Holy Trinity, Allen

*St. Brigid's Church,
Milltown*

Church of the Immaculate Conception, Allenwood

DATE OF CHURCH: 1954
ARCHITECT: CHARLES POWELL
BUILDER: A.J. CROSS
BUILDING PASTOR: FR. EDWARD O'BYRNE P.P.

St. Brigid's Church, Milltown

DATE OF CHURCH: 1817
BUILDING PASTOR: FR. JOHN LAWLOR P.P.
STYLE: BARN -STYLE

REFERENCE is made in Dr. Mac Geoghegan's listing of churches in the 1600's to a chapel at *Ballymuillen*. An old church of the Penal Times was close by.

The church prior to this one was on the bank of the canal. Locals still remember the ruins.

Built of stone, the present church's window sills are of limestone with a fluted finish. Each window has on the outside two small heads. The church was constructed by local people under the guidance of a master craftsman from Kildare.

The church had originally two entrances. The women entered through the door on the left (now closed up, but visible), while the men came through the existing door on the right. A shrine of Our Lady of Lourdes covers the left door. The window in the gable end is of cut stone and dedicated to St. Brigid. The church was modernised in 1985, and a new altar installed.

*Church of the Immaculate Conception,
Allenwood*

BISHOP JAMES GALLAGHER (1737-1751), who in Penal Times resided in Allen Parish, is buried in an unmarked grave at Crosspatrick, located in the townland of Robertstown, named after Robhartach Mac ua Cearta, a 9th century Bishop of Kildare, who was born in that area. In 1988, at the Mass Corner at the edge of Ballyteague North, a cross was erected to those who attended Mass there in the period 1676-1798.

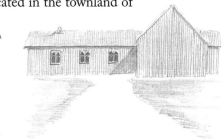

Old Tin Chapel, demolished 1952.

In 1890, the Tin Chapel in Allenwood opened for service. School was also held here 1890-1929. In 1952, this Chapel was demolished to make way for the new church. The present church is a substantial structure, built in concrete in the Gothic style.

On the 8th December 1989, the church re-opened after major refurbishment, conducted by architect John P. Delaney of Newbridge. The ceremony was performed by Bishop Laurence Ryan.

The new layout changed the seating arrangement to one of radial design around the altar - allowing for more active participation than before. The ceiling was also lowered and the main body of the church shortened.

Parish of Carbury

CLERGY IN THE PARISH IN THE YEAR 2000
V. REV. ALPHONSUS MURPHY P.P.
REV. TOM DOOLEY C.C.

CATHOLIC POPULATION: 3,000

CARBURY (*CAIRBRE O GCIARDHA*). O'KIERY, LORD OF THIS TERRITORY, WAS DESCENDED FROM NIALL OF THE NINE HOSTAGES, KING OF IRELAND IN THE 5TH CENTURY. CARBURY WAS NAMED FROM CAIRBRE, SON OF NIALL.

AT THE FOOT OF CARBURY HILL is Trinity Well, source of the River Boyne. The history of Carbury goes back to Pagan times. An extensive castle was built on the hill by descendants of Pierce de Bermingham, an early English settler.

Fiudh Wood was the birthplace of John Dempsey, appointed Bishop of Kildare & Leighlin in 1694.

Ancient churches in the parish existed in the following locations, most of which have old burial grounds: Dunfierth, Ardkil, Kilkeaskin, Kilpatrick and Kilmore.

The Church of The Holy Trinity, Derrinturn

DATE OF CHURCH: 1809
STYLE: CRUCIFORM
BUILDING PASTOR: FR. ROGER MOLONY P.P.

DERRINTURN (*DOIRE AN TSOIRN, OAK WOOD OF THE LIME KILN*)

THE SITE FOR HOLY TRINITY CHURCH was given by the Murphy family, Derrinturn, who were shopkeepers and landowners. Their landlord was Hon. George Colley, Carbury Castle.

The church is constructed of local stone with lime and sand mortar. In 1846 the roof was removed, the walls raised three feet and the present roof erected. The woodwork on the 1846 roof was done by the Mooney family of Rathmore.

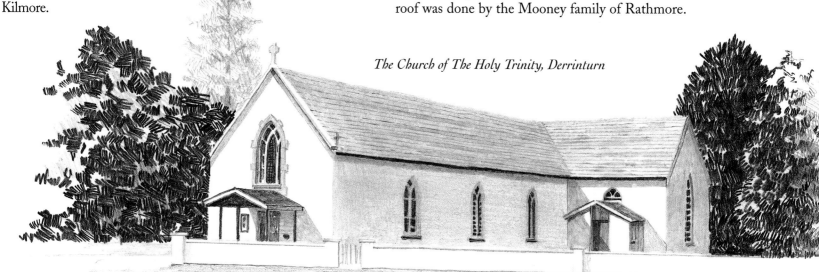

The Church of The Holy Trinity, Derrinturn

The church was renovated in 1898 and re-slated in the 1970's. There is a fine bell in the graveyard. The church features a stained glass window by Harry Clarke (1889-1931).

The church was reordered following Vatican II, during which time the marble altar, sanctuary lamp, and oil painted stations of the cross were removed.

In this church, Eamon De Valera married Sineád Flanagan of Meylerstown Hill. The family burial place of the Flanagans is in Kilpatrick cemetery where Mrs. De Valera erected a headstone to their memory in the 1940's.

Holy Family Church, Kilshanroe

DATE OF CHURCH: 1975
STYLE: RECTANGULAR
BUILDING PASTOR: FR. EUGENE S. SHINE P.P.

KILSHANROE (*CILL SEAN CUAICHE*; OLD RED CHURCH).
ON 16TH CENTURY MAPS THE AREA IS CALLED BALLYGYLCUR.

HOLY FAMILY CHURCH, Kilshanroe is a rectangular-shaped red brick structure. It replaced an old church which was built c. 1849. The site for the present church was already owned by the parish. The church was constructed by Bantiles of Banagher. The old church bell was relocated to its present position in 1975.

After the demolition of the old church in 1975 parishioners had its site outlined in stone. Decorated stones with cherubs were incorporated. Stones from Clonaugh Abbey had been used in the construction of the old church. Water fonts belonging to the old church (also from Clonaugh Abbey) are in the care of Fr. A. Murphy P.P. The wall surrounding the site of the old church and graveyard (the latter still in use) was built c. 1938 on the instructions of Fr. William Rice.

Bishop Tom Flanagan of San Antonio, Texas, is a native of Rathmore, in the parish of Carbury.

Holy Family Church,
Kilshanroe

John Duffy

Parish of Balyna

Clergy in the Parish in the year 2000
V. Rev. Michael B. O'Connell P.P.
Rev. Joseph Brophy C.C.

Catholic Population: 1,800

Balyna (*Béal an Átha*, mouth of the ford. Also thought to be derived from Ballynadrimna, a constituent part of the parish. *Baile na Druimme*, town of the little drum or hill range).

I N THE 16TH CENTURY, laws were enacted to dispossess the O'Mores of Leix and to convert the area into a shire to be named Queen's County. The O'Mores fought strenuously against the occupation and when the Plantation of Leix was completed under James I, large numbers of O'Mores and other septs were deported to Kerry, Clare, and Connaught. Calvagh O'More had previously acquired the castle and town of Balyna in Co. Kildare, previously the lands of the Delahoids.

The O'More stronghold was a place of refuge for clergy in periods of persecution. Dr. Mark Forstall, Bishop of Kildare, and first Bishop of Kildare & Leighlin, ordained priests in Balyna in 1678, 1679, and 1680. This bishop suffered terrible persecution, and was forced to live in a hovel built by himself in a marsh. He was imprisoned for some time and died in 1683. When writing to Rome, Irish Prelates used fictitious names. Dr. Forstall's was the German title M.F. Von Creslaw.

St. Mary's Church, Broadford

> Date of Church: 1856
> Style: Gothic
> Building Pastor: Fr. Felix Tracy P.P.

Broadford (*An Táth leathan*, the broad or wide ford).

S T. Mary's Church is a fine structure with interesting stained glass windows.

Fr. Mogue Kearns, from Kiltealy, Co. Wexford, was assistant priest in Ballyna prior to the Rebellion of 1798, in which he took a leading role. His endeavours to arouse the people of Balyna were condemned by Fr. Michael Corcoran P.P. Fr. Kearns and rebel leader Anthony Perry were hanged in Edenderry in 1798. A plaque to Fr. Kearns adorns St. Paul's church, Edenderry.

Fr. Corcoran moved to Kildare parish and then to Tullow, Co. Carlow, on his appointment as Bishop of Kildare & Leighlin in 1815, in succession to Dr. Delany.

St. Mary's Church, Broadford

St. Patrick's, Johnstownbridge

DATE OF CHURCH: C. 1830
STYLE: GOTHIC
BUILDING PASTOR: FR. MICHAEL FLANAGAN P.P.

St. Brigid's, Clogherinkoe

JOHNSTOWNBRIDGE,
(*DROICHEAD BHAILE SHEÁIN*; EARLIER NAME, JOHNSTOWN).

THE PARISH PRIEST who built St. Patrick's Church, Fr. M. Flanagan, was in all thirty-eight years in charge of the Parish. He was also Vicar General of the Diocese. A tablet placed over his burial place pays tribute to his years of service to his parishioners. Another tablet pays respect to Rev. James Butler, Adm. of Carlow, who died in 1860, aged 37 years. There is also a memorial window to him in Carlow Cathedral.

St. Patrick's, Johnstownbridge

The church has attractive ceiling plasterwork, and a gallery at its rear.

St. Brigid's, Clogherinkoe

DATE OF CHURCH: 1860
STYLE: GOTHIC
BUILDING PASTOR: FR. FELIX TRACY P.P.

CLOGHERINKOE (DERIVED FROM EITHER *CLOCH A RINCEADH*, THE DANCING STONE, OR FROM *CLOCH A ROINTE*, THE STONE (OR CASTLE) OF THE DIVISIONS).

ST. BRIGID'S CHURCH is an imposing structure. Of note are its stained glass windows and Stations of the Cross. It replaced an earlier church which was either built or enlarged in 1749, as attested by the inscription over the doorway - "D.D. P.P. 1749". The initials refer to Dominick Dempsey, P.P. in 1749.

John Duffy

Parish of Rathangan

PARISH PRIEST IN THE YEAR 2000
V. REV. GERARD O'BYRNE P.P., V.F.
CATHOLIC POPULATION: 2,400

Church of the Assumption & St. Patrick, Rathangan

> DATE OF CHURCH: 1958
> ARCHITECT: CHARLES POWELL
> BUILDING PASTOR: FR. PEADAR MAC SUIBHNE P.P.

RATHANGAN (*RATH OMGHAIN*, IMGAN'S FORT).
THE RATH IS NEAR THE PROTESTANT CHURCH.

THE CHAPEL OF THE PENAL TIMES, built c. 1700, stood immediately within the wall of Harberton Demesne, and is marked on a map of Co. Kildare published in 1752. The next chapel was on the site occupied by the 'old' church of Rathangan and is now a community hall. The present Protestant church occupies the site of an earlier parochial chapel.

Due to the large influx of workers to the Bord na Móna camps, it was decided that a larger church was needed. The present church is a modern concrete structure of imposing dimensions. It was built by Mr. Dick Cross and local tradesmen. The church was blessed by Bishop Thomas Keogh.

In the early 1970's it was decided to re-order the church. Mr. Richard Hurley

Early 19th century peat compressing machine

was appointed architect, and site work began in January 1976. The following artists were also engaged: Mr. Michael Biggs to design the altar, the ambo, the tabernacle pillar and baptism font, all in Dublin granite; Mr. Patrick McElroy to produce the tabernacle, sanctuary lamp, hanging crucifix and candle sticks, in beaten copper and enamel. The hanging cross measures 6ft. 6ins. in height, and 5ft. across. The altar is the church's most prominent feature, and weighs over two tons. The organ is the only item from the old church. It was installed originally in 1911 by Telford & Telford.

In 1970 Rathangan was separated from the parish of Kildare. The first Parish Priest of Rathangan was Fr. William Kinsella (1970-1982).

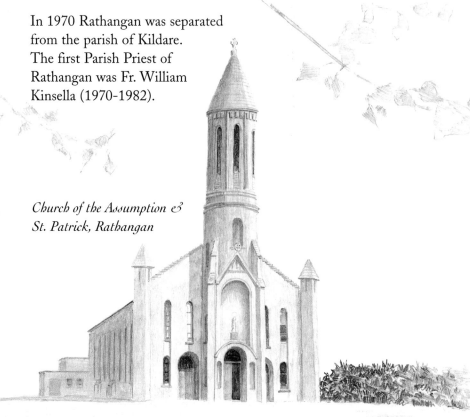

Church of the Assumption & St. Patrick, Rathangan

NAAS DEANERY

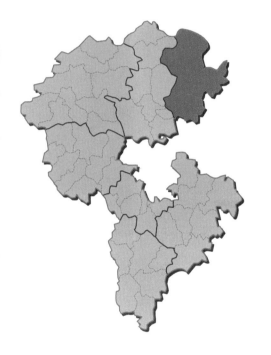

PARISHES

NAAS	112, 113
SALLINS	114
TWO-MILE-HOUSE	115
NEWBRIDGE	116, 117
CARAGH	118, 119
COOLERAGH	120, 121
KILCOCK	122, 123
CLANE	124, 125
KILL	126, 127

Parish of Naas

CLERGY IN THE PARISH IN THE YEAR 2000
V. REV. MOLING LENNON P.P., V.F.
V. REV. DENIS DOYLE P.E., C.C.
REV. JOHN BRICKLEY C.C.
REV. RUAIRI O'DOMHNAILL C.C.
REV. NOEL DUNPHY C.C.

CATHOLIC POPULATION: 12,000

Our Lady & St. David, Naas

DATE OF CHURCH: 1827; STEEPLE 1858
ARCHITECT: J.J. MCCARTHY
STYLE: GOTHIC
BUILDING PASTOR: GERALD DOYLE P.P.

NAAS (*NÁS*, A FAIR OR MEETING PLACE; THE MOST ANCIENT RESIDENCE OF THE KINGS OF LEINSTER).

ST. PATRICK visited Naas on a number of occasions and baptised two sons of King Dubhlang at a holy well in Oldtown. A manuscript poem in the library of Trinity College Dublin states that "Nás is without a king ever since Cearbhall was slain". He was the last King of Leinster to reside at Naas and died in 904.

The town was occupied during 1641 by the forces of the Lord Justices and it was at this time that the Dominican priest Fr. Peter Higgins was hanged. Cromwell's forces captured the town in 1650.

Henry VIII suppressed the 12th century Augustinian friary. A Dominican Friary was established in 1355.

The early Irish Church practised great devotion to St. David. Successive churches in Naas were dedicated to him. Fr. Denis Dempsey P.P. obtained a lease on a site for a church near the Moat, in 1755.

Work began on the present church in 1822 and by 1858 the 200ft. high steeple had been completed. Much of the interior work was done during the 1860's and 1870's.

The church was solemnly consecrated in 1949 by Bishop Thomas Keogh. Following major refurbishments which included a new roof and limestone floor, Co-adjutor Bishop Laurence Ryan rededicated the Church

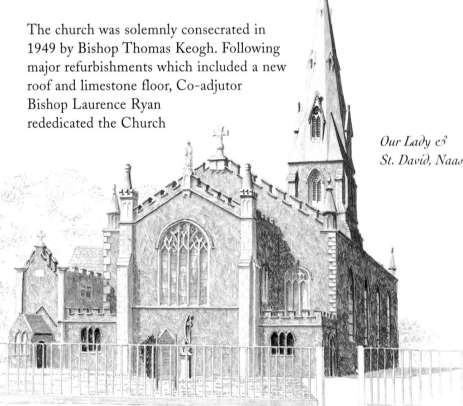

Our Lady & St. David, Naas

112

in December 1985, in the presence of Bishop Patrick Lennon.

The architect was Mr. Richard Hurley, and the following artists contributed - Benedict Tutty, a monk of Glenstal Abbey: Tabernacle and surround; Michael Biggs: Altar; Bernadette Madden: Batik; Brid Ni Rinn: President's Chair, and Lua Breen: Ambo.

Buried in the grounds in an unmarked grave lies Dr. Thomas Leverous, Bishop of Kildare 1554 - 1577. Exposed to continuous danger, he died in a poor hut at Naas, aged 80 years.

Fr. Peter Higgins O.P.

FR. PETER HIGGINS worked in the Naas area at the time of his martyrdom. On 2nd February 1642, an expedition from Dublin entered the deserted town of Naas and discovered him. Fr. Higgins was offered a choice: either to renounce the Catholic faith or hang. On the scaffold, holding aloft the document of offer, Fr. Higgins declared "This proves that it is for my faith I stand here. These men want me to deny my religion. I spurn their offer. I die a Catholic and a Dominican priest". He was martyred on 23rd March 1642.

Church of the Irish Martyrs, Ballycane

DATE OF CHURCH: 1997
ARCHITECT: EAMON HEDDERMAN
BUILDER: ELLEN CONSTRUCTION
COST: £1,800,000
SEATING: 500
BUILDING PASTOR: MOLING LENNON P.P.

AT THE TIME OF CONSTRUCTION of the church of Our Lady & St. David, the population of Naas was about 3,500. The population increased rapidly after 1970. The Church site was purchased from Naas U.D.C. for £30,000 in 1993.

The name 'Church of the Irish Martyrs' was registered in Rome in 1995. The stories of 17 martyrs are depicted in the stained glass windows of the church and include Blessed Peter Higgins O.P., of Naas, who was hanged in 1642.

The church is modern in style with brick walls over blocks of concrete. The roof is domed and the sloping floor leads to the oval-shaped sanctuary area. The beautiful stained-glass windows are complemented by the ceramic Stations of the Cross. The Baptismal font is of Dublin granite and the floor is in mosaic.

Externally the 20ft. tall Penal Cross symbolises the Penal Times when bishops of the Diocese lived in hiding in the Bog of Allen.

Church of the Irish Martyrs, Ballycane

Parish of Sallins

PARISH PRIEST IN THE YEAR 2000
V. REV. COLUM SWAN P.P.

CATHOLIC POPULATION: 2,750

Church of Our Lady and the Guardian Angels, Sallins

DATE OF CHURCH: 1923
BUILDER: LAXTONS, ENGLAND
BUILDING PASTOR: FR. MICHAEL NORRIS P.P., NAAS

SALLINS (*NA SOLLÁIN*, THE SALLY BUSHES).

SALLINS grew with the construction of the canal in the 1780's, a waterway which brought prosperity to many areas along the route. In olden times, this rural district was served by churches at Waterstown and Bodenstown. In Penal times, when priests had to register, a priest who lived at Whitechurch in the vicinity of Kill, served the district.

Sallins church was formerly a 'Chapel of Ease' in Naas parish. In 1973 Dr. Patrick Lennon constituted Sallins a new parish with Fr. Laurence Newman as first resident Parish Priest. The church is most unusual. It is a prefabricated structure consisting of a metal exterior, and a totally wooden interior. It was purchased in and brought over from England. It is similar to British Army churches, and presumably came from the same source.

The stained glass windows, presented by the Boushell family, Naas, are by Meyer of Munich. The finely carved wooden altar was presented by Anne Conlan. The stone crate font came from St. Bride's church at nearby Waterstown, and was in the custody of Naas parish until 1995. It is to be placed in the church as a Baptismal font.

A silver chalice found in a garden in Sallins is now housed at Naas. It is inscribed "Pater Joannes Mac Sihi me fieri fecit Anno Domini 1685".

In June 1798, the rebellion in Kildare ended when, following a meeting with General Wilford at Sallins, a truce was agreed, and William Aylmer and other leaders surrendered. Ceremonies take place annually at nearby Bodenstown to commemorate Theobald Wolfe Tone, a founding member of the United Ireland movement in 1791.

Church of Our Lady and the Guardian Angels, Sallins

Parish of Two-Mile-House

PARISH PRIEST IN THE YEAR 2000
V. REV. J. BRENDAN O'BYRNE P.P.

CATHOLIC POPULATION: 900

St Peter's Church, Two-Mile-House

DATE OF CHURCH: 1790
STYLE: CRUCIFORM
BUILDING PASTOR: FR. NICHOLAS FLOOD P.P.

TWO-MILE-HOUSE TAKES ITS NAME FROM A HOUSE AT MYLERSTOWN CROSS WHICH WAS TWO IRISH MILES DISTANT FROM NAAS. TWO-MILE-HOUSE FORMED PART OF NEWBRIDGE PARISH. IT BECAME A SEPARATE PARISH IN 1981.

IN THE 1600's Dr. Roche Mac Geoghegan lists Killashee as a parish church in the Deanery of Naas, and Stephenstown in the Deanery of Clane. An ancient church exists at Herbertstown, and its old Baptismal font and holy water font are preserved at St. Peter's Church.

Ruins of Herbertstown Church, built c. 1490. Mathias White of Mullacash, who died in 1789, was the main benefactor of St. Peter's, leaving £200 for the building of a new chapel at Two-Mile-House. Archibald Hamilton Rowan (1751-1834) donated the site. This liberal-minded gentleman was a founding member of the United Irishmen in 1791.

St Peter's was built in what was open countryside at the time - no village existed and neither Newbridge nor Naas had a church. It has balconies in the nave and transepts. The stone used came from a quarry at Mullacash belonging to one Charles Lewis. The original belfry was built mainly of granite, from Ballyknockan, Co. Wicklow. The 1856 tabernacle was replaced by a new one in 1974. Reconstruction work took place in 1965, following the discovery of dry rot.

The church has one of the oldest examples of stained glass in Ireland signed "J. Sillery, Dublin 1818", and depicting St. Peter. The church contains several beautiful stained glass windows, including two by Joshua & Harry Clarke, Dublin.

In the 1970's artist Mr. Ray Carroll redesigned the elements in the sanctuary.

St Peter's Church, Two Mile House

Parish of Newbridge

Parish Team in the year 2000

V. Rev. Joseph McDermott P.P.
Rev. John Dunphy C.C.
Rev. Liam Morgan C.C.
Rev. Seán Maher C.C.
Rev. Ned Murphy O.P., C.C.

Sr. Maureen Fitzgerald
Sr. Eileen Murphy
Sancha Magat
Karl Bergin

Catholic Population: 20,000 approx.

St. Conleth's Church, Newbridge

Date of Church: 1852
Style: Early Norman Gothic
Building Pastor: Fr. Timothy Kavanagh P.P.

Newbridge (*An droichead nua*; refers to the crossing on the River Liffey, near where St. Conleth's church stands).

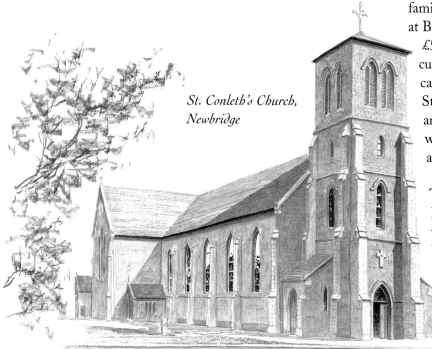

St. Conleth's Church, Newbridge

The area of Old Connell was noted for the art of metalwork from Pagan times. One skilled in this craft was St. Conleth who resided there as a hermit. He came to the attention of St. Brigid and, on her recommendation, was appointed first Bishop of Kildare, and assisted her in looking after her convents and monasteries.

In 1816, a Cavalry Barracks was built, following which Newbridge greatly increased in size. Fr. Timothy Kavanagh P.P., appointed in 1837, set about building a larger church. He secured a site on the north side of Eyre St., but before work had begun, a more suitable site was donated by the Mansfield family, where work began in 1847. The stone for it was quarried at Boston Hill near Rathangan. The parishioners contributed £500 but this sum was expended on site work alone. A new curate, Fr. Patrick Carey, was an excellent fundraiser - he even canvassed the gentry at the 'Curragh Meeting'. Originally St. Conleth's was an oblong structure, consisting of a nave, choir, and sanctuary. The stained-glass window in the right transept was the gift of J. O'Donohue Esq., of Rosehard House, and shows full length figures of St. Brigid and St. Conleth.

The church was enlarged during the pastorates of Fr. Martin Nowlan and Monsignor Thomas Tynan, who installed stained-glass windows by Meyer of Munich. When Mgr. Laurence Brophy was pastor the church was solemnly consecrated by Bishop Matthew Cullen in 1929.

Cill Mhuire , Ballymany

St. Eustace's Dominican Church, Newbridge

> DATE OF CHURCH: 1966
> ARCHITECT:: PATRICK CAMPBELL

Cill Mhuire , Ballymany

> DATE OF CHURCH: 1982
> ARCHITECT: JOHN DELANEY, NEWBRIDGE
> BUILDER: TERRY McGOFF, NAAS
> SEATING: 800
> BUILDING PASTOR: FR. LAURENCE NEWMAN P.P.

BALLYMANY (*BAILE NA MANACH*, TOWN OF THE MONKS). THERE MAY HAVE BEEN A MONASTIC SETTLEMENT IN THIS AREA CONNECTED WITH ST. BRIGID OF KILDARE.

AROUND 1904, the ruins of the "Capella de Ballemanny" were found on the Murphy farm at Ballymany. The Capella was pre-Norman, suggesting that there was indeed a community of monks in this place. The site corresponds with the location on Taylor's map of 1783 showing a Protestant church.

In Cill Mhuire laminated beams span the roof, carrying traditional slating, and the roof slopes gently to a point over the Sanctuary. The beams are supported by concrete columns and a sense of intimacy is conveyed by the sloping floor. To the rear of the main church is a day chapel which seats 50 people.

The stained-glass windows are by Lua Breen, a past pupil of Newbridge College, and show themes from Psalms 148 and 149. The new "hangings" in the church are by Helena O'Keefe and were added in Year 2000.

IN 1253 the Dominicans established a house at Athy and, in 1355, one at Naas. Although now in Newbridge, the house is officially recorded as 'the Convent of Naas'.

Suppressed in 1541, the Naas Dominicans moved to Yeomanstown, parish of Caragh, later they built a mud cabin on the Commons at Newbridge which afterwards became a permanent residence and, on Christmas Day, 1819, they opened a church . This church was replaced in 1870. St. Eustace's is the third on this site. The stained-glass by Murphy & Devitt shows themes from the Book of Revelation. The Stations of the Cross, carved from bog yew, the Crucifixion Group and Altar Panels, cast in concrete, and the Madonna & Child in polished limestone are the work of Fr. Henry Flanagan, O.P. The statues at the entrance, representing St. Dominic and Blessed Peter Higgins O.P. are also by Fr. Flanagan.

Blessed Peter O'Higgins O.P. martyred 1642.

St. Eustace's Dominican Church, Newbridge

Parish of Caragh and Prosperous

CLERGY IN THE PARISH IN THE YEAR 2000
V. REV. JOHN O'CONNELL P.P.
REV. THOMAS MCDONNELL C.C.

CATHOLIC POPULATION: 3,500

Our Lady & St Joseph's, Caragh

DATE OF CHURCH: 1960
ARCHITECT: CHARLES POWELL
BUILDER: ANDY CROSS
BUILDING PASTOR: FR. JEREMIAH BENNETT P.P.
STYLE: GOTHIC
COST: £57,000

CARAGH (FROM *CARRACH*, A ROCKY PLACE.
IRISH *CARR, CARRAIG*, A ROCK STANDING BY ITSELF).

THE OLD NAME FOR THIS PARISH was Caragh & Downings, the latter being approximately three miles from Caragh. An old church ruin exists here and is thought to have been connected with St. Farnan.

The old church at Caragh was probably built by Fr. Anthony Higgins, P.P. in 1790. In 1875, Fr. Augustine Kinsella became P.P. He was a brave defender of the people at a time when evictions were rife and he served time in jail for his agitation. Michael Davitt heard Mass in this old church when on his way to the meeting at Clongory, which established the Land League Plan of Campaign.

The Church of Our Lady & St. Joseph has a 100ft high Anglo-Norman tower. This is capped with a slated pinnacle and is flanked on either side by a cone-shaped chapels which contain the Baptistery and Mortuary. The main door features Celtic moulding. It was opened by Bishop Thomas Keogh in May 1960. From the 1790 church came six small stained glass windows which are incorporated in the Baptistery and Mortuary chapels, and a granite cross now marking the grave of Fr. Jeremiah Bennett.

Inside the church is a plaque honouring Fr. Jeremiah Bennett P.P., (1954-1987) on the 70th anniversary of his ordination in June 1996. He died in 1997.

Cross From the Old Church marking the grave of Fr. Jeremiah Bennett

Our Lady & St Joseph's, Caragh

Our Lady & St. Joseph's, Prosperous, Co. Kildare

Our Lady & St. Joseph's, Prosperous

DATE OF CHURCH: 1869
STYLE: GOTHIC
BUILDING PASTOR: FR. DENIS FURY P.P.

IN 1780, Prosperous was established by Robert Brooks as a centre of cotton production along the Grand Canal north of Naas. In less than three years a town of 200 houses had been built and named 'Prosperous.' Within twenty years the looms had ceased production - casualties of a war-time depression.

On 23rd May 1798, the rebels attacked stations where troops were billeted and killed Capt. Swayne along with some 60 of his men. By the end of the Rebellion, the village of Prosperous and the church were in ruins.

The church of Our Lady & St Joseph occupies a site where at least one earlier church existed. It is a fine limestone stucture. Major renovations took place in 1972/73 under Fr. John Gahan C.C.. In Nov. 1973 Bishop Patrick Lennon performed the opening ceremony. A further general restoration took place in the 1980's under Fr. Pat Dunny C.C. and architects Messr. McGrane and Partners. The main contractor was Algard of Newbridge, while Gallagher-Hagger of Dublin built the new roof. The restoration was enhanced by the tapestries by Miss Cathy McAleavey. The rededication ceremony was performed by Fr. J. Bennett P.P., assisted by priests from neighbouring parishes. Relics of three saints were inserted in the altar-stone: St. Oliver Plunkett, St. Teresa, and St. Maria Goretti.

The church has a chalice dated 1770, a gift to the parish of Downings, and a 15th century baptismal font from the old church of Killibegs, which was moved here in the 19th century. It is octagonal, bearing an angel holding a shield.

The Prosperous Crozier
In the 1800's the Prosperous Crozier was discovered in the Bog of Allen. Dating from the early 13th century, it is of brass and is highly ornate, although some of the original stones are missing. It is 4ft. 6ins in height and is currently housed in the museum of Clongowes Wood College.

Parish of Cooleragh and Staplestown

CLERGY IN THE PARISH IN THE YEAR 2000
V. REV. PATRICK RAMSBOTTOM P.P.
REV. ERIC CANTILLON S.J., C.C.

CATHOLIC POPULATION: 1,500

THE PARISH OF COOLERAGH AND STAPLESTOWN WAS FORMED IN DECEMBER 1971, AND HAD PREVIOUSLY BEEN PART OF CLANE PARISH.

Christ the King, Cooleragh

DATE OF CHURCH: 1962
ARCHITECT: A. LARDNER & ASSOCIATES
BUILDER: JAMES GERAGHTY, CELBRIDGE
BUILDING PASTOR: FR. JOHN DOYLE P.P.
SEATING: 500

COOLERAGH (*CÚL RÍ*, KING'S CORNER). WHERE 'REE' FORMS PART OF A NAME IT GENERALLY MEANS THAT THE PLACE WAS CONNECTED WITH SOME GOVERNMENT INSTITUTION OR PERSON.

THE PEOPLE OF COILL DUBH attended services at a temporary oratory located at a pipe factory in the Bord na Mona camp at Timahoe until the new church of Christ the King at Cooleragh was completed.

The site for the church was donated by Mr. Robin Cusack. The church is built in modern style and is simple but very dignified. It is a portal framed structure with a concrete tiled roof and exposed block work as an internal feature. It has a plain marble altar and a tabernacle of marble and bronze. A large baldacchino hangs over the altar. Stained-glass windows depict St. Brigid and St. Conleth (Patron Saints of the Diocese), and St. Patrick. On the Gospel side, at the entrance to the choir gallery, is a 30ft. by 7ft. stained-glass window depicting each of the twelve apostles. The sanctuary has a 30ft. by 10ft. window depicting Christ the King. The Stations of the Cross are made from broken stained-glass chippings and arranged in mosaic form.

On the day of the opening, Mgr. James J. Conway, P.P., V.G., commented that "this is a lovely church, modern yet devotional, artistic but not bizarre". The Sanctuary was re-ordered about 1970.

Christ the King, Cooleragh

John Duffy

St. Benignus, Staplestown

> DATE OF CHURCH: 1750
> STYLE: CRUCIFORM

STAPLESTOWN (*BAILE AN tSÉIPÉIL,* TOWN OF THE CHURCH).

ST. PATRICK, on entering Leinster between Cloncurry and Kilcock, is reputed to have stayed at Druim Uirchaille, present day Dunmurraghill. This location was an important monastic settlement up to the time of the Danes and the close of the 9th century. St Benignus is said to have been a son of the King of Leinster who chose to follow Patrick and who was renowned as a singer, musician and raconteur.

This tradition implies that the present church is in continuity with a mission established by St. Patrick or his followers. The building has three galleries. Until 1829, it was rectangular in shape.

On May 24th, 1798, the barracks at Prosperous was attacked by rebels and about 60 occupants killed. The next day troops burned the thatched church at Staplestown. This church had been built c. 1750 and, in the course of rebuilding, three courses were added to the walls and a slate roof put on. The church was enlarged in 1829 to cater for a growing population, when extra floor space in the nave and transepts was added, and the galleries made accessible from the outside by stairs. In 1939, the church again needed repair. Fr. Laurence Kehoe, P.P. of Clane, asked parishioners to contribute £1,200 towards a cost of £2,000, to repair one of the oldest churches in the Diocese.

In the late 1960's and early 1970's the sanctuary was re-ordered in accordance with Vatican II.

Once again, in 1994, the people contributed to the refurbishment of their church. The roof was fully insulated, walls were plastered, and carpet laid. The church was rewired and painted internally and externally. New lighting and public address systems were also installed.

St. Benignus, Staplestown

John Duffy

Parish of Kilcock and Newtown

CLERGY IN THE PARISH IN THE YEAR 2000
V. REV. P.J. BYRNE P.P.
REV. PAUL O'BOYLE C.C.

CATHOLIC POPULATION: 3,500

St. Coca's Church, Kilcock

DATE OF CHURCH: 1867
ARCHITECT: J. J. McCARTHY
STYLE: EARLY GOTHIC
COST: £10,000

KILCOCK (CILL COCA, CHURCH OF ST. COCA).

KILCOCK lies on the Rye Water between Kildare and Meath. St. Coca, also called Ercnait, foundress and patroness of Kilcock, lived in the 6th century. Legend has it that she was a sister of St. Kevin and was St. Columcille's embroiderer.

St. Coca's Church, Kilcock

Dr. Richard O'Reilly, P.P. of Kilcock, became co-adjutor bishop of Kildare & Leighlin in 1781. In 1782 he became co-adjutor bishop of Armagh. He died in 1818 as Archbishop of Armagh.

Between 1854 and 1859, Fr. William Treacy P.P. purchased plots of ground at Boherboy, now Church St., Kilcock. This was to become the site of the church of St. Coca. The former parish church stood on the site of St. Joseph's Hall, School Street.

The church of St. Coca was begun in 1862 by Fr. Treacy, who had spent £1,000 on it before he died that year. Construction continued under Fr. Thomas Geoghegan P.P. and in September 1867, Bishop James Walsh consecrated the church. It consists of chancel, nave, and aisles, with a tower 108ft. high. The church's total length is 131ft. and it is 60ft. wide. The nave is separated from the aisles by six bays with arches resting on granite pillars. The altars are of marble and Caen stone. The fine stained-glass windows are the work of L. Lobin of Tours, France, installed in the period 1892-1898.

Fr. Thomas Geoghegan (P.P. 1862-1889), completed St. Coca's Church.

In 1975 the church was reordered. In 1998, a radio system was installed to broadcast services to surrounding areas.

An icon of St. Coca is a recent addition to the church. It was blessed by Most Rev. Laurence Ryan in 1999. It owes its imagery to Dr. Chris Morash, N.U.I., Maynooth, and was the work of Sister Aloysius McVeigh of Derry.

John Duffy

Church of the Nativity of Our Lady, Newtown

Monument at Croppy Grave, Ovidstown.

ERECTED IN 1948
BY THE
OVIDSTOWN COMM. COM.
TO THE MEMORY OF
THE MEN OF 1798
WHO ARE BURIED HERE

DATE OF CHURCH: 1975
ARCHITECT: RICHARD HURLEY
COST: C. £70,000
RENOVATION ARCHITECT: EAMON HEDDERMAN

NEWTOWN (*AN BAILE NUA*).

BALLYSCULLOGE / SCULLOGESTOWN, ("the small farmer's town"), was an ancient parochial district which is now part of Kilcock parish. The first reference to a church in the area occurs when Roger de Hereford gave it to St. Thomas' Abbey, Dublin, in the early 13th century. In Dr. Mac Geoghegan's list of ancient Church sites, Scullogstown is listed as *Ecclesia de BallynaScolloigy*.

The site of an early parish church exists in Hortland, the demesne purchased by Rev. Josiah Hort, 1745. In building his mansion he used stone from the old church. This explains why no trace of the building remains. The church which pre-dates the present modern structure at Newtown was built by Rev. William Treacy in 1840, at a cost of £3,000. In the early 1970's architect Richard Hurley discovered extensive dry rot and advised that the only economic solution was to demolish the church and build a new one. The project began in 1973, by which time the expected cost had risen to £70,000. In 1975 the old church (except the tower) was demolished. On St. Patrick's Day 1975, Bishop Patrick Lennon opened the new church.

The year 2000 saw major renovations and extension works carried out at a cost of £600,000. The church was blessed and reopened by Bishop Laurence Ryan on 12th May 2000. The architect was Mr. Eamon Hedderman, Dublin, and the main contractor was Mr. J.V. Ledwith of Dunboyne, Co. Meath.

Parish of Clane

CLERGY IN THE PARISH IN THE YEAR 2000
V. REV. DENIS HARRINGTON P.P.
REV. PAUL DEMPSEY C.C.

CATHOLIC POPULATION: 5,400

St Patrick's & St. Brigid's, Clane

DATE OF CHURCH: 1884
STYLE: NEO-GOTHIC
ARCHITECT: WILLIAM HAGUE
BUILDING PASTOR: FR. PATRICK TURNER P.P.

CLANE (*CLAON ATH,* THE SLANTED FORD).

CLANE had a monastery in ancient times and Colgan refers to a church at Clane prior to the middle of the 6th century. St. Ailbe lived here for a time, and presented his cell to St Senchell, who later founded a monastery at Killeigh, where he died in 549. In the year 1162, a synod of the clergy in Ireland was held at Clane, attended by 26 Bishops and many Abbots. In the 1200's, Sir Gerard Fitzmaurice, second Lord of Offaley, founded a Franciscan monastery at Clane. In 1839 the Presentation Convent was established. Forty years later the Sisters kindly offered their garden as a site for the new church. The building was dedicated in 1884, in a ceremony performed by Bishop James Lynch. The limestone came from Mr. Marmion's quarry and cost 6d. per ton. (This was probably Matthew Marmion, uncle of Blessed Columba Marmion). Granite came from Ballyknockan, Co. Wicklow. The proposed spire was never built.

In 1993, a new roof was installed. In 1998, a new Baptistery was added.

St Patrick's & St. Brigid's, Clane

John Duffy

Sacred Heart, Rathcoffey

> DATE OF CHURCH: 1710
> STYLE: CRUCIFORM

Archibald Hamilton Rowan (1751-1834)

RATHCOFFEY; Coffey's Rath or fort. The hill was a central gathering point on the high road leading from Tara to the kingdom of Leinster.

Rathcoffey was the residence of the Wogan family, the first of whom, John, Lord of Picton in Pembrokeshire, arrived in 1295. Three Viceroys of Ireland were Wogans.

Archibald Hamilton Rowan, United Irish activist in the 1790's, purchased Rathcoffey Manor from Richard Wogan Talbot of Malahide. He levelled the old castle ruins and built a fine mansion on the site.

The church of the Sacred Heart is a small stone structure with balconies on either side of the altar. Entry to these is by means of granite steps on the outside of the building. It was remembered as originally having a thatched roof.

It was built in 1710 by Lady Frances Jennings, wife of the Duke of Tyrconnel, Viceroy of Ireland. She was a Wogan of Rathcoffey. Her husband had died during the Siege of Limerick. She is reputed to have gone to France before the Duke's death. She returned to Ireland and joined the Order of Poor Clares at King St., Dublin.

Rathcoffey church is reputed to be the oldest Post-Reformation Catholic church in Kildare & Leighlin.

In November 1974, following its re-ordering, the church was re-dedicated to the Sacred Heart by Bishop Patrick Lennon. The church was completely refurbished in 1997 at a cost of £86,000.

Sacred Heart, Rathcoffey

Parish of Kill

CLERGY IN THE PARISH IN THE YEAR 2000
V. REV. WILLIAM O'BYRNE P.P.
V. REV. MATTHEW KELLY P.E., C.C.

CATHOLIC POPULATION: 3,300

St. Brigid's Church, Kill

> DATE OF CHURCH: 1821
> DATE OF EXTENSION: 1970
> STYLE OF CHURCH: BARN-TYPE

KILL (*CILL*, CHURCH) REFERS TO *CILL BRÍDE*,
THE CHURCH OF ST. BRIGID.

CEARBHALL, the last of the Christian Kings of Leinster, who resided at Naas, was slain in battle in A.D. 904 and buried at Kilcorfain (supposed to be present-day Kill).

The Registry of the Abbey of St. Thomas, Dublin, which contains records of land grants to the Abbey in the 13th century, provides the earliest mention of St. Brigid's Church in Kill, when Thomas de Hereford gave to the Abbey his churches of "Kill and Thrillerdelan", (now Castledillon near Straffan).

The site of the medieval Catholic Church of Kill is now occupied by the Protestant church. Many Catholics are buried there, including two previous Parish Priests of Kill, Rev. John Doyle and Rev. John Andoe. The chapel preceding the present church stood in the nearby townland of Hartwell. A pathway leads from this place to a holy well named after St. Brigid.

The present church was built by Rev. Daniel Nolan P.P. (1804-1822). It was refurbished in the pastorate of Fr. John McDonald in 1970 when an additional wing was built, and the old part of the church was re-roofed. The new wing was a dual-purpose construction, separable from the old Church by a screen. It serves as a meeting place for the Parish and can be converted for the purpose of worship at week-ends. Thus the seating designed for the new wing was adjustable, to face in two directions. Notable features are the tower with its raised coigns and pinnacles and the dressings around the windows - all of Wicklow granite. The entrance consists of cast-iron railings and impressive stone pillars.

A new presbytery adjacent to the church was built in 1999.

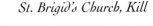

St. Brigid's Church, Kill

126

John Duffy

St. Anne's Church, Ardclough

DATE OF CHURCH: 1985
ARCHITECT: MR. PAUL O'DALY AND ASSOCIATES, DUBLIN
BUILDER: MCLAUGHLINS & HARVEY
COST: £350,000
SEATING: 300
BUILDING PASTOR: FR. PAUL MAHER P.P.

ARDCLOUGH, NEAR OUGHTERARD IN KILDARE; *ÁRD CHLOCH*, HEIGHT OF THE STONES; STONY HEIGHT.

THE SITE FOR ST. ANNE'S CHURCH was donated by Mr. & Mrs. Michael Costello.

The church was built in 1984/85 by a church committee chaired by Mr. John Molloy, and was blessed by Dr. Patrick Lennon on the 19th May, 1985. The new church replaced a church built on the nearby canal bank.

The building is of striking angular construction and design. The roof of slates is steeply pitched and incorporates high level patent glazing. The building is of steel frame with walls of simple napper plaster. The timber-sheeting ceiling incorporates louvres which diffuse the natural light, while the floor is of natural quarries which together convey a feeling of harmony and balance. The lighting arrangement emphasises the sanctuary area.

The stone in the front wall and gateway of the church is a link with the past, having come from the "Smithy" at Clonoughlis. This "Smithy" is very old and appears on all maps of the area. The bell came from the old church at Lyons and has kindly been presented to the parish by University College , Dublin.

St. Anne's Church, Ardclough

John Duffy

127

Bibliography & Alphabetical Index

Bibliography

Brenan, Martin, *Schools of Kildare and Leighlin A.D. 1775-1835* (Dublin, 1935)

Carville, *Geraldine, Abbey of the Three Rivers* (Kildare, 1984)

Carville, *Geraldine, Monasterevin: Valley of the Roses* (Monasterevin, 1989)

Comerford, *Rev. Michael, Collections Relating to the Dioceses of Kildare & Leighlin*, 3 Volumes   (Dublin, 1883-1886)

Costello, Con, *Kildare - Saints, Soldiers & Horses* (Kildare, 1991)

Hennigan, Ken & Nolan, William (eds.), Wicklow: *History and Society* (Wicklow, 1994)

Harbison, Potterton, Sheehy; *Irish Art & Architecture from Prehistory to the Present* (London 1978)

Joyce, P.W., *Irish Names of Places* (Dublin, 1869)

Kee, R., *Ireland - A History* (London, 1980)

Lecky, W.E.H., *A History of Ireland in the 18th Century* (U.S.A., 1972)

MacLysaght, Edward, *Irish Life in the 17th Century* (Dublin, 1979)

Mac Suibhne, Peadar, *'98 in Carlow* (Carlow, 1974)

McEvoy, John, *Carlow College 1793-1993 : The Ordained Students and Teaching Staff of St. Patrick's College, Carlow* (Carlow, 1993)

O' Hanlon, Canon John and Rev. E. O'Leary, *History of the Queen's County*, 2 Volumes   (Dublin, 1907-1914)

O'Toole, Jimmy, *The Carlow Gentry* (Carlow, 1993)

O'Toole, Jimmy, *Carlow's International Achievers* (Carlow, 1999)

Packenham, Thomas, *The Year of Liberty : the story of the great Irish Rebellion of 1798* (London, 1969)

Price, L., *Placenames of Co. Wicklow* (Wexford, 1935)

Small, S., *An Irish Century 1845-1945* (Dublin, 1998)

Swayne, Seán, *"The Old Grey Mouse" Graignamanagh remembered* (Graignamanagh, 1995)

Williams, Jeremy, *A companion guide to Architecture in Ireland 1837-1921* (Dublin, 1994)

Much assistance was provided by local historians, clergy, and parish publications produced by dedicated groups of people and individuals.

Alphabetical Index

Abbeyleix	68	Ballon	27	
Allen	104	Ballyadams	64	
Allenwood	105	Ballycane	113	
Ardattin	25	Ballycommon	94	
Ardclough	127	Ballyconnell	31	
Arles	16	Ballyfin	74	
Askea	14	Ballylinan	17	
Askinagap	40	Ballymany	117	
Bagenalstown	52	Ballymurphy	43	
Ballinabranna	57	Ballyroan	69	
Ballinagar	85	Baltinglass	36	
Ballinakill	66	Balyna	108	
Ballinkillen	53	Bennekerry	15	

Borris	42	Knockananna	39
Bracknagh	86	Knockbeg College	12
Broadford	108	Leighlin	56
Cappincur Oratory	94	Luggacurren	65
Caragh	118	Mayo	18
Carbury	106	Milltown	105
Carlow Cathedral	10	Monasterevin	102
Carlow College	12	Mountmellick	80
Carmelites (Kildare)	97	Mountrath	72
Clane	124	Muine Bheag	52
Clogherinkoe	109	Myshall	50
Clonaghadoo	81	Naas	112
Clonaslee	83	Newbridge	116
Clonbullogue	86	Newtown (Carlow)	53
Clonegal	28	Newtown (Kildare)	123
Clonmore	30	Nurney	103
Cooleragh	120	Old Leighlin Cathedral	58
Croghan	91	Paulstown	54
Curragh Camp	100	Portarlington	76
Daingean	92	Portlaoise	60
Derrinturn	106	Prosperous	119
Dominicans (Newbridge)	117	Raheen (Laois)	70
Doonane	18	Raheen (Offaly)	85
Drummond	47	Rath	79
Drumphea	51	Rathangan	110
Edenderry	88	Rathanna	44
Emo	78	Rathcoffey	125
Glynn	46	Ratheniska	61
Goresbridge	55	Rathoe	26
Graignamanagh	48	Rathvilly	32
Graiguecullen	20	Rhode	90
Grange	25	Rosenallis	82
Grangecon	37	Sallins	114
Hacketstown	38	Shanahoe	71
Johnstownbridge	109	Skeoughvosteen	49
Kilclonfert	93	St. Mullins	46
Kilcock	122	Staplestown	121
Kildangan	103	Stradbally	62
Kildare	96	Stratford-on-Slaney	37
Kildare Cathedral	99	Suncroft	101
Kildavin	29	Talbotstown	33
Kileen	17	The Heath	61
Kill	126	The Hollow	73
Killamoate	39	Timahoe	63
Killeigh	84	Tinryland	22
Killenard	77	Tullow	24
Killeshin	21	Two Mile House	115
Kilquiggan	31	Tynock	34
Kilshanroe	107	Vicarstown	63
Kiltegan Fathers	35	Walsh Island	87
Knock	67	Wolfhill	64